A Rushed Quality

A Rushed Quality

David Odell

punctum books ✶ brooklyn, ny

 A RUSHED QUALITY
© David Odell, 2015.

http://creativecommons.org/licenses/by-nc-sa/4.0/

This work carries a Creative Commons BY-NC-SA 4.0 International license, which means that you are free to copy and redistribute the material in any medium or format, and you may also remix, transform and build upon the material, as long as you clearly attribute the work to the authors (in a way that does not suggest the authors or punctum endorse you and your work), you do not use this work for commercial gain in any form whatsoever, and that for any remixing and transformation, you distribute your "build" under the same license.

First published in 2015 by
punctum books
Brooklyn, New York
http://punctumbooks.com

punctum books is an independent, open-access publisher dedicated to radically creative modes of intellectual inquiry and writing across a whimsical parahumanities assemblage. We solicit and pimp quixotic, sagely mad engagements with textual thought-bodies, and provide shelters for intellectual vagabonds.

Cover photos by Gilles Forcheville, with permission of the artist.

ISBN-13: 978-0692426562
ISBN-10: 0692426566

Before you start to read this book, take this moment to think about making a donation to punctum books, an independent non-profit press,

@ http://punctumbooks.com/about/

If you're reading the e-book, you can click on the image below to go directly to our donations site. Any amount, no matter the size, is appreciated and will help us to keep our ship of fools afloat. Contributions from dedicated readers will also help us to keep our commons open and to cultivate new work that can't find a welcoming port elsewhere. Our adventure is not possible without your support. Vive la open-access.

Fig. 1. Hieronymous Bosch, *Ship of Fools* (1490-1500)

TABLE OF CONTENTS

//i

Preface

//1

A Rushed Quality (2000)

//171

Bodying Forth (2002)

//307

Select Bibliography

Preface

These texts belong neither to philosophy nor to poetry—and yet they are for the most part focused on a substantial area of overlap between these two venerable disciplines, vis-à-vis the question, "What is it like to be X?" Philosophers like to fill in the X with something exotic like a bat or a dolphin, or even an Artificial Intelligence, while poets tend to fill it with something else, equally exotic, namely themselves. For the diffident and introspective author of *A Rushed Quality* and *Bodying Forth*, the X, while definitely human, is perhaps someone in general, equally distant from and equally intimate with both the writer and the reader in the very moment of their eponymous activity.

It is often observed that things come into focus for a brief time during the transition between two epochs of a life, whether individual or collective. Once the new dispensation is established, one looks back with a certain nostalgia at that strangely shimmering lucidity encountered on the hinge. All that might remain, as in this case, is a series of snapshots with a clear enough sequence, but no real beginning or end. Of the transition here, we can only say that it concerned a different feeling about embodiment and about time, and that these were quite ordinary effects of the accumulation of lived days.

The start of it all was the perception of what was called the "rushed quality," as something persistent and bothersome and of which there was no question of its ever being shed. Rather than evaded or denied, it was welcomed because it seemed for the first time since childhood to mark a structural occurrence presenting a new metaphysical datum.

As it happened, this quality proved very elusive in its mature bothersomeness and the inquiry into it soon turned into a sort of quasi-theoretical fascination, which took as its main theme the fate of pure subjectivity—the utterly unfunctional, utterly useless, utterly dispensable feeling of being. The rushed quality is perhaps merely the sense of it draining away, or its long-sustained decrescendo. In this it has proven to be more than a merely personal accident, but a cultural indicator as well, pointing in the direction of a number of striking developments—a sort of technological enframing of subjectivity, its willing assimilation into massive networks, the giving over of metaphysical subjectivity to quasi-scientific discourses, and the concomitant explosion of ethical subjectivity —all facts that the author of these pieces was not yet in a position to confirm, indeed not even to ask himself how Walt Whitman's "Song of Myself" might read in the age of the "selfie."

But the self is also an extraordinary power of recuperation, of rising again and again from its own ashes, and this power was very much in view, and especially in relation to its two main antagonists, one of which was named heteronomy, and the other unnamed, which we might now call syncope. These correspond roughly to the psychological and the neurological unconscious.

On the other hand the two texts presented here, whose composition was separated by a substantial period of time, can be seen as two phases of movement with respect to this initiating quality, an in-breathing and an out-breathing.

There are a number of ideas that run through many of the pieces, motivating beliefs of the writer, such as the inexhaustability and ungraspability of the moment, the existence of a direct connection to reality which is betrayed in every attempt to formulate it, and a skepticism about the bad infinities latent in the natural attitude. And of course there is a continued dialogue with various more or less identifiable thinkers and positions. But again, this is not philosophy, the arguments are virtual, and the stakes are something entirely different.

Each of these pieces emerged in a renewed relation to the blank page. It is hoped that for the reader, apart from any resonances they may set in motion, they retain some of the qualities of silence, expectation and impossibility that gave birth to them.

David Odell, 2015

A Rushed Quality (2000)

I   This rushed quality to life may continue on now, accelerating until the final fall into death. Imagine there was one more chance to step back and take a look at it all. An utterly personal investigation, unhindered by the projections and expectations of others.

2 Words are from this mind. The personal tone is chosen but not necessary, and doubtless only of limited adequacy. There are many beliefs making up this mind, or the associated person—how they will perform, what they will do, what the value of their gestures is estimated to be.

3

Moments when it can speak, can express the limits of its meager understanding, are rare and brief. "It would be good to stop time, to reach into the timeless underpinning of one moment, right down into the generative core so that all future moments could be justified." That is what it thinks, but when it acknowledges it to be impossible it shrinks back and gives over to appetites and its own phantoms of desire.

4 Many different voices and stagings arise here, or they seem to, because there is always a sense of confusion about where this line of thought should go, and what should follow it. As if I am being tested against reality, and not any sort of big reality—just this personal, small, one life of a reality, this inexhaustible and banal here and now.

5 Subtract away vanities of the mind, the heart, and the spirit, even vanities of the body, and what is left over? Who or what could still speak in that final and first place? I, he, it, the mind, the speaking: all equally inadequate.

6 There is no way to measure these vanities, but even here the speaking is guarded and hesitant, half stifled. At other times there were abundances, and how good it felt to unburden myself of these. Even if I were alone there was the sense that speaking this could do something for someone. What I call vanity is the memory of past beliefs.

7

So, I'll be walking down the street and the contraction—the sense of looking at the world through a jerky pinhole, and of great physiological cycles in the body that cut each thread of thought so short—will be upon me, almost unbearable. And yet I'll know that I'm knowing this, whatever that may mean, and that somehow if this separable awareness was speaking itself then all would be redeemed.

8 Knowing even the failure to know, in this failed knower. The emptiest of all categories, and yet I seem to have lived only for that.

9 That words, that knowing, that some inner act could make a difference: this is what seems to be demanded, yet you know that this could not be so. How can I reach you and touch you once and for all, how speak from behind the tapestry, yes, here, once and for all?

10 To put this impossibility before me each day, to pray to it before I go to bed at night and to kiss it each morning; the metabolism doesn't allow it. Once or twice a year it returns, like *Brigadoon*.

11   Here, with a sickening abundance, are all those moody images from my solitary life. The little habitual perceptions that are not registered as habits. Myself in my life, in the bodies of my ancestors, doing this human thing, day after day. Evocative snapshots, at least so conceived. But if I find anybody else doing it I become irritated, "No, not that!"

12 To distill the essence of this melancholy consciousness, because it seems that this distillate is an object that would always be alive. Many times I've looked at this from the outside and seen it as a form of trickery, a knotted promise with no substance. And now from inside it, that demystifying gaze seems incomprehensible, or at least premature.

13

From a formal point of view, it has certainly been distilled many times before: to all intents and purposes, the same subjectivity shimmering nacreous on the page. On countless other pages. That, of course, is precisely the spur here: to do it again, yet differently. The same reflexes, the same complex moves, back and forth, the shuttle stroke, in order that the reading stand at a point equidistant from the showing and the hiding.

14 The romantic consciousness, the self in time, the glancing flash of liveliness: that sheer energy that would shatter all restraints, that speaks itself in the poetical word, and transforms the speaker to at least the limits of humanity. And then the inundation and exhaustion of this movement, in every conceivable way. Like a fire spreading into every line of tinder, in every conceivable way. And then new and seemingly inexhaustible, energyless echoes of this same movement, repeating ad infinitum. Fractal consciousness.

15

A text is an operator of consciousness, and implicitly I assert that I am its fixed-point. A contraction operator, as irony can be here understood, is known to always have such a fixed-point. That's reassuring.

16 Is there any such thing as consciousness? It is a word that simultaneously makes certain things possible and forecloses certain others.

17

The understanding that "this, here"—*Dasein*—is a consciousness knowing itself through knowing what is not itself, seems to be one of the big contexts. Perhaps there is just one other, viz. "From the beginning, not a thing is." The former, however, does not depend on the auxiliary concepts of a self, or of doership. There is a certain independence from what passes, even if it is passive, and a questing through "experience," passing through, for what it is but does not know it is.

18 The dimensions of the questioning engendered by these paragraphs, the readerly, the writerly: each of these is of course plural. The former taking place, say, in a rapid and not particularly sympathetic perusal, and as such forming a part of the background for the writerly, which includes both the days and weeks of composition, filled with other things, and the intervals when there is the experience of unformed sentences, of reaching out over gaps, the living of this. The mysterious presence miscalled consciousness seems equidistant from all these fields.

19

It can appear that a life is questioning here, and to put it this way merely invokes a number of special reflective spaces and metaphors. It could have appeared as something quite certain, yet what is actually present is an uncertainty, looking to attach itself to the facticity of handy cues. So, call it a life or a consciousness, or a history, a psyche, or even by another name; it is essentially the same thing.

20

Such inquiries would be merely academic were it not for the fact that the experient of life, the passenger, under whatever guise it falls, has this theoretic core. When you look at all that is known or hypothesized in its bearing on this present moment, there is a vast overlapping contextual structure, and by theoretic injections one may find oneself located in any part of it, as virtually that part itself. It is a weak sense of location, however, since it dissolves before any rigorous demand.

21

Chasing this phantom passenger as far as possible out of idealistic redoubts, it arrives at the edge of an abyss. The theoretic nature of the subject shelters a demand, and when this demand is apprehended nakedly at the limit of theory, one finds it peculiarly un-shy of the abyss. The demand is not theoretic. How can this be? How can there be a question beyond the possibility of the concepts that could formulate it? How can there be another knowing, ungraspable in any theoretic net? The answer is laughably simple when the question is formulated the right way.

22 What kind of event is this, here, now? A moment of embodied consciousness, an instant of a life, of its unfolding, a tiny pebble in the history of the universe. None of these. All of these. There is something strange in the difficulty of even formulating this question.

23

Accept that there is nothing in the phenomena immediate to this apprehension of the question and of its difficulty that indicates the answer, or even whether the question is meaningfully posed. The thought mechanisms, we are told, were designed for something else. Yet all of that is grist to the mill. Our aim is precisely to make strange; the strangeness is both question and answer, at least provisionally.

24 If there were some kind of disembodied continuation of life after death, an astral plane or some such space, then would we sleep and dream there? Presumably not, since there would not be the physical body or brain to be fatigued. And so the kind of self we would experience would have little in common with what we know now. Similarly with any other physically bound aspect of life. The kind of life lived there would have so little to do with this one that it might as well be someone else entirely.

25 This elusive awareness—can it be thought in any way apart from some subtle concept of an apprehension of the whole, or the pure potential of such an apprehension? All such concepts are seen to be founded on typical illusions, continuities whose field of operation is exclusively belief. If there were, in fact, continuity, we would not recognize ourselves. The alternative is pure and systematic negation, but what passes for this is (generally?) only an idea of it, in thrall to the same belief in consciousness.

26

There is something salutary and ethically stimulating in taking in the evidence of the discontinuity and heteronomy of the ideal subjective realm, the working correlative of "the self." Is it that this complex idea is structurally, but non-logically, a function of its own negation? That would make it a sort of "self" within the "self," amongst other infinite regresses. So, there may be a sort of sublime and virtual Subject of the entire sceptical, scientific explanatory enterprise. It is theory and the self is theory, but the self was theory first!

27

Primacy of awareness, or this virtual and transcendental Subject, or Truth as an act, an unveiling, a recognition, a lifting of the forgetting: how this idea pops up again and again in various guises, even after it was thought to have been dismissed. It does not much differ from a correspondence theory of truth—that a pure receptivity can conform itself to the simply seen, which seems to be necessary to ground the enterprise of wanting to know, even if this enterprise is "seen" to be futile. Taken purely as a functioning, the enterprise in which "truth" is a token (amongst others) is in no position to demand anything, much less correspondence to something. It proceeds as long as the thinking has not yet collapsed into some singularity in logical space.

28 If there were correspondence as a central function, then we would be more able to be sympathetic with each other. Learning would be easier, not so dependent on experiencing for oneself; it would be possible to convey the sense. As it is, our efforts in these directions show the patterns of creative but hopeless misunderstanding.

29   There is an underlying question here which I have been thinking about for more than 20 years, when I have been able to do so, but it is difficult to formulate explicitly. Is the atom of consciousness homologous (in any way) to the "natural" consciousness as theorised from everyday experience (folk psychology?), or is it radically strange and not like "consciousness" at all? "Atom of consciousness" being understood in the least question-begging way possible.

30 When it is written out like this, the question seems a crazy one. For whom could this possibly be an issue? Which experient could embrace both poles with sufficient detachment? But perhaps this question veils yet another, even less easy to formulate and possibly even more crazy, since it is segregated from criticism, or even clear scrutiny. Such a question has the potential to give rise to numerous commentaries, and somehow we expect these to articulate with the concerns of others, but perhaps we are each so isolated within the field of our own obsession that we readily hallucinate such articulations. All of which would be an example, of course, of the very strangeness that the question seeks to address.

31 The medium scale of experience: this means the here and now but with acceptance of all working abstractions that are at hand. Does it exist at all? Perhaps it only seems to in retrospect. In any event, it seems to know itself, irritably, as incomplete, as lacking any solid grounding and therefore unable to rely on its own constructions from one moment to the next. The micro- or atomic scale is when this question of a ground is attempted to be ferreted out, and the macro- or historical scale is where the opposite of ground, which is irony, is given maximal weight.

32 Rightly pursued, commentary on the phenomenological core of the experient can bring about interesting changes in the reading consciousness. It suggests that the Being of this event, whose parameters are otherwise quite unknown, can be at issue. In a positive sense, this Being names the pure space of potentials differentially activated "here," the operator whose selective eigenvalues are all that is known. The positive sense must always lead to error, to mistaking the species for the genus. That Being is at issue cannot be taken in any light way. As a reality, it cannot be any sort of special event; it is the only event, a contradiction in terms.

33 There is a far more elusive side to this event, at least for this writer—to speak from within the emotional representations as they arise without falling into any of the errors of over- or under-credulousness. Sometimes the speaker is outlined against the sunset or dawn, his hand raised in some rhetorical gesture, but the more reliable manifestation is this shrinking away into apparent emptiness, this disingenuous sense that of course there is nothing much to say here.

34

The responsible self is the one in time, acting, responding, measuring in time. But what is this famous time? It is all too easy to slip away from in this writing since the words do not belong to the same temporality. What medium sustains the dimension of "my life"? What evidence is there that something recurs?

35

Of course, it might be possible to wake up from this remembered life and see that it was only a dream after all. The only evidence that it could be otherwise is the vividness of the present, and this fails entirely. It is quite possible to imagine a super-present against which this one, known as the invariant reality of "life," would seem quite thin and shadowy. That is because the present is a sort of project for being, and without presuming that it could ever be completed, one can imagine it at a far more advanced stage. If one extends this imagination and tries to include the metaphysical shell that it carries, snail-like, as we carry some version of Kant's categories, it seems that it could be infinitely different from anything we know.

36 The "la vida es sueño" is culturally overdetermined. It may express an incapacity to live or a satiety with life. It may be suspended in the heat of action, but it is always a possibility once that action is complete and is reflected upon.

37

Big metaphors for life, such as "a journey" or "a dream," may be meaningless in themselves since there is no reference point outside of life from which to expose them, but they have a different use in that they raise the very question of such a reference point. More than that, they seem to awaken a knowledge that just such a viewpoint has always existed. This "seeming" is a very interesting one, since it may point to the paradoxical logic of the concept of life as a sort of self-referential concept—that is, intentionally self-referential but extensionally not so. Or else, it may indeed point to a grounding awareness, an ineffable and radically present space of possibility.

38

Life is like a dream, because in calling it "life" we admit that it is already a story, something told, or, in the telling, already an adventure in interpretation. There is a sense that however spontaneously it is lived, life is erected upon a broad flow of happening, such as cannot be named prior to experience, yet that out of which experience is sculpted. Contemplating this, the idea arises that there is no flow, no time, no space in this pure underlying happening. Again, how does this idea arise? Is it the paradoxical logic of quasi-self-reference which generates such a strange topology, or does the topology point to something implicitly known, like one of those sensory figures, or homunculi, where the body parts are shown in proportion to the size of their mapping in the sensory (or motor) cortex?

39

While I cannot say that I am the body, I also cannot say that I am not the body. The apparent knowing of the latter is an artifact. Part of the "I" function in ordinary awareness is "I am not the object"; it is the way the mechanism works. Thus, by successively enumerating the parts of the body, one may verify in turn that the virtual subject is other than the composite virtual body—that is, the body as posited by thought, language, imagination etc. This proves nothing at all. If the real body were absent then there would be no one to carry out the inquiry.

40 Strange figure of speech: "my life," and its variants. Not quite the same as "in my experience," since the former implies the totality and the one for whom there is this totality. At what point in the development of reflexive language does it become necessary to incorporate the concept, implicitly or explicitly uttered, "my life"? The move to transfinite concepts.

41 Is this related to the possibility of saying, "life is a dream"? It seems that there are many other localities of meaning in the living of "a life" which have equal or greater authority as implicit judgements to "life is like a dream"—usually in the midst of some passionate activity, when it is not an explicit reflection but a fullness of living that temporarily resolves the doubt about whether this is yet "life," a doubt which one didn't know one had until that very point.

42 The idea of transfinite concepts: just as the mathematics of the simplest physical movements, or of more complex but unremarkable ones like riding a bicycle, are immensely complex if explicitly developed, so it is with the structure of naturally inhabited concepts. It is not to be assumed that just because they are logically complex they are recondite or rare.

43 It is only on certain occasions that there arises the desire to adequately speak the moment, yet it seems at those times that this is the truest desire. That imperious phenomenology is what proves it is desire, just as does the reflection that the adequacy that haunts it has never been and can never be achieved. It is a phantasmatic filling up, with meaning this time. And yet, the speaking happens—all too finite, but strangely sufficient.

44

A thought is a representation without intrinsic ground. That is, it is a picture without any assurance that the context that makes that picture possible is an ultimate one in relation to the apparent contents. The absence of intrinsic ground is what makes it possible for thought to be usefully local, as well as to chain together in diverse and unpredictable patterns. This very thought is itself a perfect example of what it describes. But why is it that there should even be a question of grounding?

45 To be aware that one is thinking is itself just another thought, and yet there must be an irreducible moment of acknowledgment for it to be possible. It is unclear whether this is a logical conclusion, or some other kind. What can be said of that moment of acknowledgement? It can't itself be represented, yet it is "experiential," even if it cannot be framed as an experience. Understanding that this is an essential but necessarily overlooked aspect of "experience" implies a vastly different global representation of "experiencing" or "living."

46

Any kind of attention brings about a structured phenomenology, not just in the objective phase but also, by a strange implicitness, in the subjective phase as well (even though, by definition, the subjective phase is invisible in any single act of attention). This seems quite remarkable, because it suggests that even the barest attention is already theoretically structured to seem like just that. Attention is just an idea, and if it weren't so suspect, we might be tempted to say that both the subject and the object in any act of consciousness are objects to some unnameable Subject.

47 What of that "strange implicitness"? In knowing X, through sheer attention and compresence, my organ of knowing is felt to be myself. I am available, wherever needed, to fill the vista opening out by whatever of X is revealing. I am this availability to know correlative to X's availability to be known. And what was meant by "myself" just now? As soon as the idea comes of this knowing of X, a frame forms around it, and I am outside this frame. X reveals only one more of my accidents, and in this sudden alienation I seem to know myself more fully, but negatively. X is now seen again as the essential catalyst of this moment, non-separate from its unity. This works as dialectics, but does it do as well as erotics?

48 Dialectics, in the broadest sense, speaks of homologous structures found in many localities of experience, many different enframings. Some of these frames are harder to abstract than others, so it seems that awareness of the homologies may be of assistance in doing so. There may be a mathesis for translating a lived understanding from one region of experience to another, from a clearly delimited frame to one that is largely *horizon*-al and ungraspable.

49

The nodal points of a dialectic, as understood in this way, are terms such as self and other, subject and object, awareness, horizon, ground, etc.: all the terms in the broad family of phenomenology. Again, awareness of the homologies—as between, say, a movie or a poem and one's own self-understanding—suggests a dialectic of dialectics; it is not that the structural patterns are the same, but that what is deep and unspeakable is that which seems to glimpse its face in these fleeting reflections. The glimpsing and the seeming, these are equally terms of a new movement framed within its deep negation.

50 It is difficult to observe the transition from sleeping to waking; the dreams seem to become more frenetic, and the first superventions of the awareness of day are merged in with them, with the failure of the dreaming mind to be able to maintain its dream, let alone give it some sort of conclusion. The first waking moments are fuzzy with a bland acceptance, and consciousness reclaims the body without any sense of an other to make some metaphysical contrast. The dream melts away from this diffuse and intuitive body like a mirage.

51

What is the right question to ask about direct experience? Not, "Show me direct experience," and not "Is there direct experience?" The first presumes absurdly that it can be indicated, the second that it has being. "Does experience presuppose an event that neither is nor is not experience?" is perhaps better. There is almost a logic that demands a positive answer to this question—that is, not a logic, but a persistent mirage of a logic. Of direct experience we must also affirm that, in so far as it may be spoken of, at no moment is it unknown. The question then arises, "What kind of event is the supervention of speakable experiencing?"

52

Life is a dream: meaning not that it is thin and illusory like a dream, but that it is thick and overdetermined, that events unfold unpredictably and yet with an uncanny and insistent pertinence and a strange dream-like solipsism. The press of overdetermination produces a kind of wandering development with sudden state-changes, which in turn produce the illusion of illusion. You are a character in my dream as I am in yours, so where do we meet? Or should I say that that we do meet is event beyond the dream in the dream?

53

When I write the word "here," it can refer to the space of this writing as it is being brought forth, or it can refer to this life, this space of experiencing and referencing. In each case the word gives consistency to something that would otherwise seem more uncertain in its unity and possibly opaque to any reference. It has to do with the continuity of thought, the thought that makes this utterance, being itself a discontinuous phenomenon. In the latter case, the fact that it has a beginning and an end gives a unity to subjective space that is not apparent in its contents.

54 As in set theory, it is impossible to comprehend the universal class, although it can be implied by an appeal to mere being, which is perhaps no more than a verbal indication. The facts of a beginning and an end, birth and death, go beyond this correspondence, since they delimit the most universal frame—what I call the first world. Here, what is meant by birth and death are, however, not the same as the empirical events occurring in historical time. Their certainty does not derive from the overwhelming weight of precedent; it is encountered in the very core of the search for understanding. It is inseparable from the making of meaning.

55

What is the topology of awakening? It is not the dreamed character that awakens, clearly, but it is also not the dreamer, since the two functions of dreaming and awakening are incompatible. It sometimes seems as if dreaming is nothing but a continual failed awakening, so that the dreamer is the failed awakener. To be in the state of waking up is to be in a certain situation which is in its own way as dramatic and insistent as the dream, but there is something wonderful in the transient awareness of two worlds, roughly similar in nature (spatial, embodied, locally narrativised, etc.), but of such non-compossible reality. This is only a transient awareness; soon the waking state becomes its own sort of failed awakening.

56 I called it failed awakening because it seems as if the objects that most persistently draw attention and even desire are somehow projections of the whole space, and thus pointers to the way out of it. They necessarily fail to lead one out because, however well they point, they are still in the space of the dream. Even the dialectic of such objects is itself such an object. This is only a certain way of seeing them, however, predisposed by a deep-seated "gnostic" presupposition.

57

The first world is not an experienced world, nor is it just the logically presupposed reality behind any world-experience. It is nonetheless a world, and that is why it is intimate with this ontological finiteness, insusceptible to proof. The first world stays the same when local worlds, when all completed meanings, supervene on each other. There is no meaning and no subject in it; it is what is not constituted in any way, but all constitutions presuppose it. No matter what happens or fails to happen, we never leave the first world. This knowing, freed in all its parameters, all its suppositions, all its knowingnesses, returns to the first world as a musical composition returns to its home key.

58 Yet there is no one at home in this firstness. There is no one also to say what became of the one. The one is never superceded, and yet it has vanished. The one is with others in a meeting that abandons phenomenology and its logics. So perhaps it could be said of the first world, "We are," and yet it is still uninhabited.

59

Knowing finds its only fulfilment in the first world, but there is no knowing there because there is no knower. The starkest kind of differencing, without any point from which to make a distinction. What becomes of knowing? Who knows?

60 This mapping of the first world does not belong to the first world. It belongs, perhaps, to the mapping world, and by the very same gesture, by the very same maps, it gives rise to the many apparent spheres of the neurotic world.

61

It seems easy to show that we can never get hold of reality. All the mechanisms available for any such a getting hold are always limited in scope, and reality is independent of scale. For example, the concept or the word, which are fine as functioning on an immediate scale but absurd on the scale of, say, the "world." Mathematical and scientific techniques seem far more successful, but even they only function in carefully delimited contexts. Why is there this urge, then, to be in alignment with reality?

62

The urge itself and the activities it gives rise to—which from a certain broad perspective are a large part of what we do—can seem deluded, yet it is precisely this revulsion from known delusion that drives us back to it. To see that all positions are false is itself a position about positions that we take to be true. Perhaps there is only this negative knowing, but then we seek the rigor of this negativity.

63

I am walking along the street, my eyes are taking in the scene, understanding is rapidly processing everything that momentarily fills my attention. It is very lively; it is what is happening. It is human consciousness and so it only assumes its reality in the space of all active human consciousness, in this moment. This space is inconceivable: not just the number of humans and the plurality of visions—even to know one other is too much. As a specific human consciousness, everything positive, every specific difference potentially experiencable, falls into this immense totality. To be in relation to this totality (which is radically unknowable in positive terms) is the same as what it is to be aware in this moment, that implicit *ekstasis*. To be aware is precisely what is not awareness of any content(s), but it can in no sense be pointed to in this way.

64

The whole precedes the parts, and it is the implicit reflection of the whole in the part that makes the part possible as part. The parts form an explicit reflection of the whole, as their object, but limited by perspective. The parts disagree as to content but agree about those aspects of their reality (the categories) that follow from its perspectival nature. It is this that they call reality, and it forms the basis of the elements which they assemble in order to gain a knowledge of the whole.

65

These thoughts are like the bubbles in my lava lamp: slow-moving, short-lived, sequentially repeating with indefinite variation, and dimly reflecting each other on their opalescent surfaces. From the top of the column of water to where the bubbles rise filled with heat, there is rarely any merging. They have an identity, a skin, and they gently jostle against each other to gain the highest point before they cool and redescend. At the bottom, there is always a mother pool that swells and gives birth to endless fresh bubbles. They rise and the pool is depleted until old bubbles return and merge with it. This moment of merging is marked by a tiny shock-wave that travels over the now continuous surface. Alternatively, when a rising bubble separates from the mother pool, it stretches and thins the neck between them. The elongated neck breaks in two places and a small perfectly spherical bubble forms and hangs poised in the interspace.

66 Something seen becomes a metaphor for the system of the seeing. How did it arise that there is a one who demands this knowing? Desire goes out but fails to fulfill itself and so it turns back to merge again in its source. But it is deflected on the way back, since it cannot retrace its steps exactly, and so instead it adopts the source, via a reflection, as its new object. The nature of desire is to be mercurial, ever changing and adapting, and also to be of a strange dual nature, both pure phenomenon and latent structure, so no matter how oblique the motive embodied, it always seems transparent to itself.

67

The "I" fails to be an I, therefore it is an I. Or, the subject fails to be a subject, therefore it is a subject. Or, self-reflection fails to reflect itself, therefore it is self-reflection. There are a few ways in which this might be understood. It could be that the failure itself is the negative medium in which there is enough formal self-reflection to underwrite the pure project of a subject, or an I, or whatever. Or it could be that nothing on the level of the I or of any other performance (in thought) could, or even needs, to guarantee the subject. These are masks through which the reality manifests, and it is precisely their failure that makes them able to function as masks. That which they present can be presented in no other way, so they are "it" at the level of presence.

68 It is strange that post-phenomenological philosophy has so much currency. Perhaps it is strange about any philosophy, but here, these ways of declaring the pre-conceptual nature of what happens seem to be dredged up from a very particular and personal contemplative space, yet are instantly recognised by the reader as his own, even if the language is quite opaque. One's own most intimate thoughts are found to have been anticipated by some professional philosopher somewhere, and then shortly afterwards they have filtered into art, and then are everywhere taken for granted. But post-phenomenology is also a game. We know the landscape very well, but who can penetrate deepest into the cave with a syntax and grammar thought to be far too large for the opening?

69

This, here, ineluctably recognised as a kind of suffering, but for which the words won't come. How to speak of this very poverty of spirit? There is a kind of condemnation that does not want to admit this state or anything about it, and it, the condemnation, has free reign it seems. It is extremely personalised, it contains the very pseudo-essence of privacy, and yet one knows it to be broad enough to be a sort of sociological condition.

70

This willful suffering, then, has something in it of the quixotic desire for uniqueness. This desire is incoherent and groundless (almost like, but in other ways quite opposite to, the desire for truth; what family of motivations does that freak of nature spring from?), yet preserves itself from that knowledge by a general clouding up of the mind. One cannot be unique in knowledge anyway; the closer affinity is with pain, which seems the prime datum of apartness.

71

How does it come about that there is an experiencing of suffering? On what medium has it grown? It is as though the screen of experience can tilt through various angles in space-time. When it has a tilt relative to the time axis, then there seems to be a flowing, a working out in time. Any grasping of the predicament so revealed entails an entire mechanism that sustains that tilt. This is a buried history of mistaken living that forms the implicit preconditions for the ongoing story: the parameters that maintain the frame. Everything, including every mode of self-understanding that falls within the frame, partakes of the same essence of becoming. Even the constitutive differences in temporality are synchronised.

72 At the end of a cycle, the voice that sustains this writing faded and was lost in the background noise. On looking back, it is seen that the thoughts do not repeat themselves as exactly as was expected. It was rather the insistence on haste that meant that it was impossible to follow up most of the pathways of inquiry that fleetingly opened. The tracks do not go through a wood, but an urban kaleidoscope. But it is often difficult to face what comes directly in my path. At the conclusion, the cycle faded on the ungrasped notion of the finite.

73

This seems to be a spontaneous reporting, a simple telling, and yet it is known also as a rare physiological achievement. When conditions are right, when there is a certain permission, then time can be folded back to make the vantage point which is spoken for. I mean to say that everything that is said about "life" is uttered or read by an agent of such a precariously achieved system, it is a function of operations quite heterogenous to its internal self-understanding. It surfaces from the mute purposiveness of organic life, for example, and what it "sees" is coloured almost entirely by the clash of its discursive pre-conditions and its "real" conditions. Real is parenthesised because it is not knowable if it can even be indicated in this way. Discursively, there is only an indicial space in which such operations as "precondition" are natural and productive.

74

To see psychic or spiritual life as some sort of function of reality, so that it arises with no essential connection out of the extended void. It pursues its intrinsic development in oblique relation to this real, growing in internal complexity through mastering the hazards and contradictions necessarily engendered by its own progress. It feeds on energies and organised differences that come from outside itself, but which do not have to undergo any change in nature to nourish it, since it always already assumes them to be of its own substance. Not interpretation, but pure "pretation." Eventually these sources of difference dry up and this autonomous life-understanding goes on a long journey of decline back to the original void. This paradigm is the familiar evolutionary perspective. Here we see that it arises naturally out of the concept of "function," since this in turn implies beginning and ending, maximum and minimum, energy exchange and so on.

75

In this perspective, understanding always falls short. All possible understandings contribute no more than a system of models of reality, and the things we can be most certain of are only upwards absolute propositions—that is, if true now, then true in any larger model, but still limited to models. What is the typical logical form of the upwards absolute proposition? Own-truth in the moment. And so, reciprocally, affirming own-truth in the moment as the only form of certainty underscores the uncertain form of a world of models.

76

Generally I have accepted some such form of argument against scepticism as knowing that you don't know, or that you may not know is nonetheless a knowing. It may be empty of content, but it establishes the subject in an uncompromising position oriented towards the empty space of knowing. This is a version of a number of similar moves all based on the being of the Subject. One cannot logically convert contingency into necessity, but these categories do not apply to the being of the subject, since even though it may well be contingent, it is prior to the experience of necessity and so in a de facto sense is more necessary than necessity itself. The content of understanding can gain no warrant even from the Subject who appears to ground the opening to (the question of) preconditions.

77 The Subject is subject to the fallacy of displaced necessity; an agent that can comprehend necessity need not itself be necessary even though it is *de facto* prior to the necessary, and even though its priority is necessary as well.

78

Why the petulant tone? Who are you trying to convince? The attempt to find a language that assuages the knowledge of heteronomy. In other words, I do not presume to be capable of knowing reality, but I wish to go as far as I can on the strength of the negative: to be oriented towards the place that truth would occupy if it were knowable. You have not answered my question; why do you want that? Even that is enough to give rise to some peace of mind amongst these ever changing conditions. But this is still wanting something for the sake of something else. It seems that it is not so much peace of mind you want as security in your position—but can anything known, any attainment, give that security? Better to say that I want the truth because I haven't given up on the truth game, which is a competitive game with other "thinkers." The trouble with all this is the assumption that there is any such intention in the language of what any subject wants.

79

Why is this "knowledge of heteronomy" so taken for granted? It is not simply reality testing, but a knowledge of being, as it were, marbled with otherness in the deepest grain of living. "Shadowed by a sweetly false identity" in the fullest sense. This seems to be an immediate datum, but isn't it just the melancholy of scholars? There are even some scholars who argue fervently against it, but I am separated from them by an impenetrable and transparent screen of irony.

80

There is no such thing as mind, and when I use this word I refer to a sort of short-hand grasp of reality—an awareness of compressing the mass of data by a process of selection and representation: i.e., metonymy. Example of mind: when the plane takes off and I look down at the cityscape spread out below me I can still construe this as the city for me, part of my world, even though it is purely abstract, vision only. There is no way of reconnecting what I'm seeing to the fullness of sensory and imaginative experience—even if the plane were to crash. It is like paper money. Most of our experience in the world is necessarily of this order, so that we may navigate such complexity. This is mind: the banks are always in doubt—the currency changes, or is not interchangeable, or is rendered meaningless by inflation.

81 Metonymy, especially synechdoche, has always appeared to me the most sexual of tropes; conversely, sexual desire itself seems to be a performative synechdoche. Romance is thus metonymy pretending to be metaphor.

82 Furthermore, there is no such thing as consciousness. Where could one find the evidence that consciousness exists—in any sense? There is a sense of contrast with what is not consciousness: the body, or sleep. These accompany us all the time, but one cannot find the line that separates these from consciousness—cannot, properly speaking, even find grades of consciousness; all are equally phenomena. Actually, even if there were such a line, or such grades, we necessarily could not find them. Such is the nature of ... of, well, consciousness.

83

Mind: experience of differences—of different contexts (e.g., "pictures," "dreams," "movies," "stories," "realities," etc.). The ability to make the adjustments needed to move through these: this requires or implies comparison, memory, and a sense of being the same one in the midst of passing conditions. The evidence for such transition is difficult to rationalise; the paradoxes of change and continuity are as old as Parmenides. One can take up a different way of seeing all of this—from the point of the present, anamorphically—but it entails a violence to the ordinary language of things.

84

The structure of the world implies some parameters of order—a definite underlying topology to the understood cosmos. There is a shape to things, a metaphysical shape, but that only by virtue of being the obverse side to what is necessarily implied by perception and conception. As in Frieden's physics, the parameters of order might emerge as the solution to certain equations, as the reality that is required by general conditions of possibility. Second order equations with two independent solutions: the standard and the non-standard. One has its chief singularity at the origin, and the other at infinity. Isn't that just what we see?

85

Mountains and rivers: "the subject is an infinite task and the moment by moment failure of completion gives rise to the world as we know it" vs. "Subject is equivalent to the (infinite) posing of a question, which may simply be taken to be always already solved." The answer could never be known either way, so the only significant difference is in how the "mystery" is regarded. Rigorously follow through on the implications of this. Now we have a truly finite world. It turns out that the infintary escapement mechanism of meaning was unnecessary. Mountains are mountains again.

86

It is a law of appearance that no worldview can be decisively proven true or false. What sort of mechanism is needed to bring this effect about? Or, does it show how much hedging there is even at the deepest layers of mind?

87 This process of simply looking, to see how it is just here, is disingenuous. One way of testing this is to ask, "Am I whole or a part"? In the language of pure subjectivity, one must answer whole, because no objective division can be perceived, but clearly in any effective sense a moment of consciousness is just the illuminated tip of an unknowable mountain. One gets around this by superimposing the indefinite unknown onto the equally unknown source of consciousness. There is a certain violence to this identification—one insists that the salient quality is from the side of consciousness and begins to smuggle in its kinfolk, ideas—but in fairness, it is the other side that should prevail—the one that remains silent, unconscious.

88 It is undeniable that in the last instance our weal or woe is entirely dependent on our beliefs. This is somewhere between a self-fulfilling prophecy and a tautology, but to make this into a technology for happiness is in the same degree as vulgar as ineffective.

89 "Through the iron gates of life." When this sense is most acute, the gates lead not into life—that is, Presence—but out of it, into the irremediable.

90

How much shallow and false subjectifying there is hidden under the word "seeming." Above all, reality must be seem-less.

91 What is it to have a body or to be a body? Is there any verb that applies to the relation between what changes and what does not? There are many bodies that overlap and which are in continual change. The logistical body, the pleasure body, the pain body, the specular body, the solid body, the transparent body, the abject body, the "brother ass," etc. This living, such as it comes to read or write these words, is the continual combustion of a core of bodies, like the glowing tip of a stick of incense. It is senseless to say "I am the body"; rather, look to see if any body says "I am." Neither the genitals, the heart, nor the eyes say this, although the body gushes forth from these centres with endless vigour.

92

If we are presented with an image, it is indeterminate whether this points us to the object or the subject responsible for that image. This makes more than art possible; it is the condition of even the most banal act of seeing. We can say, "there is only the seeing," but this tends to minimize the paradoxical nature of seeing, and indeed of all perception, which in every modality partakes of the same ambiguity. In space held open by this indeterminacy we can see the entire world arise, and in this we are both seer and seen.

93 Beauty, desire, and enjoyment are three forms of interpellation. The subject-object which is interpellated is brought into play by this event, and hence is always in correspondence with Other, and thus expresses a characteristic figure of alienation. The "me" of desire is the me that harbours the Other who desires. The "me" that enjoys is that which contains the Other insofar as it is ultimately me. The "me" that experiences beauty is the indifference of itself and Other.

94 What happens when we gaze steadily into each other's eyes? A short-circuiting of social space, as all the meanings this could have (and there are layers upon layers of these) are gently put aside. It is held, and in that holding the habitual constancies can blank out momentarily. A short-circuiting of metaphysical space occurs as well. An event prevails, fed by two streams of life that know each other in nameless nakedness in this indeterminacy. The other's life: utterly opaque and yet infinitely transparent.

95

The tremendous polyphony of life is overlooked when we filter it through the narrow focal field of attention. Just say that attention is like an elastic lens that faces on to an infinite event. This lens selects a more or less large, finite fragment of event and squeezes all the rest into a two-dimensional anamorphosis. The size of the focal field may smoothly change, as may the clarity or opacity of the anamorphic fringe. Any area of event that can enter the focus must first become, or have been, salient within the fringe. Focus and fringe remain interdependent counterparts, although they are far from symmetric. In a certain reduced language, they are figure and ground.

96 In introspection, it is impossible to observe anything that precisely matches this picture, and yet meditating on the picture brings about a change in the quality of consciousness.

97 Reality is appearance and appearance is reality. There is nothing else either of them could be. And yet as appearance, it is subject to a continual unfolding, self-revelation, and endless disillusionment, while as reality it never changes at all. This is sublimely unproblematic simply because reality is no longer opposed to appearance.

98 Consciousness may be likened to a parliament. Representatives of various interests—for example, feeding the body—can take the floor and general consideration be given to what they propose. Actions may be taken, or other agencies stimulated to contribute to the debate, or the subject may be changed as a different priority takes over before any specific action is taken. Debate on certain subjects may be gagged, and then it may happen that the deputies representing that interest keep up a sort of murmuring, or more, and the ongoing business is distorted by the avoidance. There is always an atmosphere in the chamber, which is the prevailing mood or emotional tone with which things proceed. This is basically the model of faculty psychology, and it is a good one as far as it goes. What is interesting is the status of various enabling fictions of the self. Is this a republic, or is there a sovereign of some sort? Or is it a bureaucratic tyranny? Belief in the self—egoism—may be a sort of rhetorical performative function akin to patriotism, or else perhaps a legalism, or maybe as little as a sentimental attachment to the debate itself, while the real business goes on elsewhere.

99

The parliament model is one where an effective unity, the state or the self, is actually constituted by the relationship or compresence of a number of agents that, individually, are of an entirely different kind of function. It is a metaphor that enables some phenomenological insight into the heteronomy of the self. In fact, this heteronomy is by its very nature beyond any such phenomenology, but that is itself a phenomenological observation. It belongs, however, to a sentimental or sublime phenomenology.

100

Bringing attention to bear upon the felt body, we discover what we have always known. This sense of the body is the ever-present horizon of all the conscious processes of which we can say that they are "ours." It is not a single sense; the fringe of awareness is in no way monological, nor does it synthesise the plural in any way. It seems to extend into the deeper core of oblivion, and so attention may move further, even into this. And it makes the same discovery at each new depth: that it was always implicitly known. In this way, one comes to a knowledge of the unconscious matrix of all felt bodies—the body proper, the *ding an sich*. Knowledge? Whatever it is, it cannot be triangulated from the ontology that belongs to purposeful consciousness. But seeing all of this, why would one even dream of doing so?

101a "The part of the mind we call self [is], biologically speaking, grounded on a collection of non-conscious neural patterns standing for the part of the organism we call the body proper."

Antonio Damasio

101b Non-conscious precisely because it is ground for even the most subtle feeling, which it enables as some kind of relationship. In the same way, phenomenologically speaking, the self is the ultimate subject or experient, and is also non-conscious since, by definition, it cannot experience itself. And yet, that there is non-experiential knowledge of the self is evidenced by our possession of the concept "Being." To make this seem less problematic, reflect on the fact that the paradigm for the signified is the felt body.

102 Reference to the body proper means signifying the self. Body proper is non-conscious, and yet this signifying act achieves its goal because body proper really is there prior to any act or referencing. This is what bootstraps a consciousness that is paradoxical to itself, since, in terms of its own sense, it requires an infinite regress of observers.

103 How long did it take for the mind to produce such a concrete metaphor for itself in action, for itself worlding as, for example, a strip of movie film? As a metaphor it is almost random, as if a heavy voice emerges from the mist and manages to enunciate, "I am something like this." Who is speaking, and can we ever again find the place where we first heard those words?

104

How does a consciousness harbour an other consciousness, which it always does, which it must, almost by definition? Not by way of the blind spot of the subject, although this seemed the natural place to look. Rather, via the absolute indetermination of every moment.

105 In the neurologist's perspective, the instances of "human life" are put together like a puzzle made of interlocking blocks. The shapes of these blocks correspond to brain structures, but subjectively to nothing we can name. Take them out one by one and first personhood and then raw subjectivity collapse like a house that is being torn down. This is the most salient premise for the material determination of consciousness, even if, for the idealist, who does not draw any boundaries around the experiment, matter itself is just a law which consciousness has given to itself.

106

All of this, interdependent and interpenetrating spheres of being—appearance, feeling, action, personhood, sociality, etc.—is laboriously assembled in each child and slowly disassembled in each dying body. It can barely glimpse the real in the name of which all of this is taking place, and it stammers about God, death, cosmos, nature, evolution, or love. At some point in this career, to tear its knowing free of such wretched anthropomorphisms and speak! Even to conceive of such a possibility is an audacity.

107 The neurologist presents a physicalist version of the Vedanta's *neti-neti* ("not this, not this"). Are you X (some brain structure)? No, since it is ob-jective. Then, let's remove it. Snip. Now, tell me, are you still here? This goes on until the eyes glaze over and not the slightest movement can answer, "Present."

108

Seeking for the minimal unit of awareness, as if for the glowing point buried beneath secondary structures that have merely reflected it, one regresses to more primitive forms of consciousness. Instead, ask what emerges when the organism is maximally activated, when all systems are at maximal potential.

109

If Man's fall was through the temptation to know (himself), then it merely images God's fall in initiating creation. The martyr is an inverse Christ. He so loves God that he takes upon himself God's sin and suffers the justifiable rage of men against the creator of their world. It is not that men are wrong to hate God for creating them; the creation is detestable precisely so that only God becomes lovable.

110 This "precisely" is characteristically masculine. Woman has a greater rage against God than man, and a far greater love for him. Her irony: she reminds man that one must first have loved in order to hate, and that only through the strength of his love could his negation be strong enough to propel him into the Godhead.

III

Why does it always seem a good thing to yet more rigorously think on the interdependence of consciousness and embodiment? Is it that we have to keep being reminded of something, failing which we drift into unsustainable vanities, or is it that only in this direction does more of the world open to us? These are diametrically opposed alternatives—the finite and the infinite, the ironic and the sincere—although they share exactly the same ethic.

112

The problem of materialism is that matter is a concept. One appeals, then, to real matter prior to any concept, but this is *ding an sich* and our relation to it is sublime at the very least. This a delicate point where others have fallen into massive idealisms; how can one remain here in the tenderest possible acknowledgement of being held in the palm of mystery?

113 Every moment of consciousness, whether waking or dreaming, has an objective and a subjective pole. The subjective poles are necessarily objective as well, although, lacking an even deeper subjective pole to manifest them, they may be unconscious objectivities, or protoselves in Damasio's terminology. The subjective poles are unified according to an unconscious concept or category into what we call self, which is both single and multifarious. In rare moments we can see that consciousness itself does not require all this process, which is pathetic in the extreme. Consciousness has fallen in love with that pathos. This explains what love is (for us) more than it explains what consciousness is.

114 The strange joy of pissing on one's own grave. What lies mouldering there, blindly giving up its elements beneath some solemn epitaph, but the mass of all that it was ever about? And the piss? Water of love free from all loving. Be that as it may, unless I speak from the grave, I am just pissing with words.

115 This most banal of states: mute, somatic, nauseous, enclosed. The very state that all ideas, pleasures, and projects offer to lead out of, and the very one they are somehow nostalgic for. A refusal of all description, all communication, all acknowledgment—the grey nothing, cool, disillusioned, moving just enough within itself to prevent any answering for itself.

116

To whom does this moment belong? If it is part of someone's life, then it and that someone lie in a finite dimension that begins and ends with nameless passivity, a dimension that always promises just because it cannot make good on any of its promises. The person is brought about by death, because only death enframes that which pertains to the person, itself utterly not pertaining to the person. And yet if there was a person, it would pertain; hence, no person, and no ownership of this moment in any finiteness.

117 This living a life, tracing out multiple pathways through bands of limitation, temporally, spatially, energetically, empathically, cognitively, etc., is what we know we know. How much else do we know but not know that we know? How far do the limits of what is too obvious to be seen extend, of what, recognising which, we are amazed that we ever could have left home in the forgetting of it? By definition, it is impossible to put a bound on this, and yet it is a profound decision even to hold such a category open.

118

"The contentions of philosophies forms strong evidence that we venture beyond the consensual critique of knowing armed only with aesthetic judgements, those quasi-objective expressions of our physiology. Similarly, the consensus establishes the status of the unknown to be only that which is answerable to its methods of questioning." And what if some of what we know, but do not know we know, is the unmotivated circularity of all this, and who we were when we ordained it?

119 A gnostic insight always results from applying pressure to that strange concept, knowing. The concept is an attempt to crystallise something of what is signified by the word "pressure" here, but more significantly it is a concept which describes a movement in which its own subject dissolves, a movement of the subject which necessarily ends with the annihilation of that subject. This is why, like all true concepts, it has no picture, and why knowing is ultimately one with love.

120

"When I die, the universe dies with me." There are as many deaths as there are universes for this to be either true or not. Who can say anything about death? It points, however, to a recognition of this very being as grounding all of being. This is not the same as to say, "Everything is, within my awareness, since only in awareness can it be known to be." Awareness, or consciousness, when closely examined, is not identical to itself; its inner precondition is always already unawareness or unconsciousness, and that is just what it is. One can say that it rests on the body proper, but since this body is to provide the ground of this very universe, being that without which nothing is, it must be of a this-ness beyond any understanding of body. Giving of being is what I most truly am, what I most truly know, without knowing that I know.

121 With what trunk do I reach within myself to feel this rumbling of being? An elephant's or a tree's, with blood or nerves or marrow—not mine, but an Other's? This sense: the genus of which all the rest are merely species.

122 Turning to death as we walk, we are at last ready to receive its gift: to live once. Even in describing this, I deny its finality. Which of "us" accepts the gift?

123 An evening walk—spontaneous memories crowd in, briefly illuminating, like distant lightning, the unsuspected vastness of the simple interior space. These hands, these clothes, this room, now in the forty-ninth year of a life, all of this, utterly embodied, utterly specific, is the knowingness. There is no stranger who observes from a vanishing point in a perspective. Modelling by perception, one mistakes consciousness for a point and its contents for objects, but this knowingness is the space identical to its own contents. The contents may unfold according to the laws of the known, such as association, and this movement runs right through the heart of knowingness; it is its freedom. This is why spontaneous memories mock our belief in linear time and try to wake us from it.

124

Imagine a plurality in which each item could be known only as either foregrounded or as an indefinite member of the background. This could not be counted, since each item could only be attended to as "one" and, when not attended to, could only be sensed as possibly co-present and inseparable but not as "already counted" or "yet to be counted." (Possibly co-present has exactly the same valence as possibly co-absent.) This is a more primordial—that is, bodily—experience of plurality, compared to which counting is positively ideological.

125 In the order of knowing rather than of perception, relations of "items" have the same salience as "items," and relations of relations and all such. There is simply no exhaustive relation which could function as a counting. The ideological aspect of rational consciousness—the essence of which is the possibility in all instances of such a counting—is like a spectral resonance, a single eigenvector of a space-like knowing among just such an indefinite plurality of eigenvectors. This simile, like the one drawn from the non-synthetic plurality of the felt body, is a going away from here in order to come back more brightly. This is the simplicity beyond complexity.

126 It is impossible to pass from linear to spatial consciousness, since passage is a linear concept. There is no one to whom it could happen because it is realised in lieu of such a one. There is a supercession, and in it, the former understanding is seen not to have ever been an understanding at all; the latter is realised to have always prevailed. What was thought to have been understanding was a kind of project, standing in for a fullness that was required, but defined to be impossible. The knowing of that impossible was in fact the only point of reality in the whole setup.

127 Although there is no logical path that leads from one frame of core self-understanding to another more encompassing one, there is a kind of transformation of truth actions which perfectly expresses it. (This could perhaps even be symbolised in the language of mathematical Category Theory.) But how is an emotional state like this one, whatever it might be, revealed as a pattern of truth actions? What I call truth actions are not the same as beliefs—at least, not my beliefs, and not quite beliefs without a believer either. It is as if I am traversed by an Other's beliefs. And not just one Other, a plurality indefinite as to time and space and region of being; in this traversal, the self is divided and offered to the multitude with painfully blind generosity.

128

Myself as a being amongst beings is the lie through which the truth of Being can first be glimpsed. The lie is known to be a lie because it cannot account for the difference that grounds the "amongst," and so it points inexorably to the non-place of Being where it is the very non-existence of difference which grounds indefinite plurality. This is strange, because in its own realm, Being is utterly undifferentiated, and yet in expression or phenomenality it is what makes distinction possible, like a tiny mote in a supersaturated solution that triggers crystallisation. And in this manifestation, that mote is found at the point where the crystallisation is densest and hence most fractured—in the centre of what is called "I."

129 When I sit at my ease and look out over some vista, landscape, or cityscape, where a play of space meets a play of surface, then imperceptibly I melt, with the myriad associations, into a deeper vista, knowing "myself more truly and more strange." When there are other people included in the scene, it works differently; I am no longer spread equally over the field of transparency and opacity. The face and the body of each person that I include gathers and bunches me; each of them holds an infinity into which I could fall—if they were open, or even if they are not—through the cracks in their presentation, through what I could loosely call their presentiment. As if to ask, "Where is the first place where 'we' can be?" and then to drop, as in a rapidly descending elevator, right out of time and space.

130   The outer limit of imagination: a new world and a new enjoyer locked in a wholly new embrace. The inner limit of imagination: this old enjoyer, stripped of all powers and presumptive rights, and the world as it has always been, just for him. The fire of life, which is not from us, feeds the journeying between these extremes. And always with just a bit too much passion, too much heat.

131 It is remarkable that we can forget our primordial sociality to such a degree that the "constitution of intersubjectivity" seems to be a legitimate question. What is the evidence for basal solipsism? We die alone, we fear others, we can never know what they are thinking much less understand them, we must study to bend them to our will, and so on. Nevertheless, all of these must be constituted on prior sociality, and it is easy to sketch out the lines. What an absurd imposture the solitary self is! It is a myth that gives consistency to our emotions, our desires, and our ignorance. And to our loves as well?

132 In all of this which does not know knowing or bounding in any way, this carrying forth of a nameless world into a formless world, there are these crystallizations, such as this writer, or this reader and their non-identity with the "I" and "you" of the grammar. In every instance it is the implied relationships that give surety to this point of thought, which invest it with a pathos that strangely ghosts an impossible—a laughable—pretence at Subjectivity. In a strange twist it is the putative metaphysical Subjectivity behind the grammatical subjectivity that gives definiteness to whatever relationships are chosen from the indefinite fringe of possibilities. But since in reality there is nothing to do this, relationships melt into their space of possibility, where each is identical with its inverse.

133 When I was a child, having discovered the strange power of spontaneous memories, I set about manufacturing them by carefully linking what was memorable in a scene with my overflowing sense of personal being. The power to do this seemed to diminish noticeably as I grew older, and from some point on, perhaps around six or eight years of age, I entered into the dispensation which has continued ever since, in which a mental self, like someone hired for the job, attempts to competently administer this personal reality. This is a response to a social and cultural complexity in which that same overflowing of being is refracted in myriad ways before returning to its source. We have never left the space of epiphany.

134 It is not whether there is or is not free will (whatever that could mean), and it is not whether there is or is not some real space of possibilities in which this, here now, lies, as some speculate; it is simply that when we construct this moment for ourselves as one that could be different, as provisional or as a means—for us— we are drawing over our eyes the veil of a false time, a false space, and a false us.

135 Between waking reality and dream reality there is this difference: that in waking reality, material things speak to us when we closely attend to them. They hold us with their gaze, whereas in dreams we wander blindly within our own gaze. What it is that material things are saying to us we do not know; it may well be that they are trying to tell us that we are dreaming. "To practice and confirm all things by conveying one's self to them, is illusion; for all things to advance forward and practice and confirm the self, is enlightenment" (Dōgen).

136 "We are dreaming," not as the answer to "What are we doing?" but to "What are we?" This is not a simple assertion but a dialectical seed, like Hegel's "Substance is Subject." Dreaming: subject and world co-arise interdependently. Reality unfolds in depth, like the petals of an endless flower. We inhabit thoughts as we inhabit our bodies, and our bodies as thoughts; they appear to flow with the prevailing conditions. The dreamer is absent. The dreaming knows dreamer and dreamed, but what forms its ground is un-dreamed of: undreamable.

137 Prior to all these fine abstractions, this humming, this strange blind presencing, this flitting of attention, this body, this kind of nesting in things, the spine, the breath, the vague tensions playing through the frame, the frames, the skin, the scalp, the smell of fingers that have worked, the itches, the general comportment in things, the forgetting of where this is, the solicitations of half-finished tasks, the reminders, the expectations, the feel of glass, the taste of water ... All these elements with no proper names that are this, now. Everything is just to be able to bring them home.

138 Formal relations always include a certain symmetry, a reversibility of agents, or an interdependence. The other kind of relation—real, temporal, bodily, finite, all too human—is radically asymmetrical. When we discover an unexpected symmetry in bodily relations, as in sadomasochism, this seems profound—a concrete metaphysics—but when we search for such a symmetry in our anguish, we are merely succumbing to the ruses of the mind.

139 "Birth is like a man riding in a boat. Although the man prepares the sails, steers the course, and poles the boat along, it is the boat which carries him, and without which he cannot ride. By riding in a boat he makes this boat a boat. We must consider this moment. At such a moment there is nothing but the boat's world. The heavens, the water, and the shore all become the boat's time, which is never the same as the time that is not the boat. By the same token, birth is what I give birth to, and I am what birth makes me. When one rides in a boat, one's body-mind and the dependent and proper rewards of karma are altogether the boat's dynamic working; the entire great earth and the entire empty sky are altogether the boat's dynamic working. Such is the I that is birth, the birth that is I."

Dōgen

140 A smokier metaphor: we are like a radio station. There are recurring programmes which give a character to the station. Each one is a "show," a kind of presencing and responsiveness, but with its own style, its own self-reference, its own kind of nostalgia. Presenters come and go, and although shows may outlast the presenters they too go, in time. And in time, even the character of the station changes, sometimes unrecognisably. The management changes, the audience changes, the advertisers change, but it is still the same station, transmitting on the same frequency. Here, so many different paths intersect, so many different agendas, different causal streams. They meet up in a certain way and a "show" arises. It goes on for a while and seems to its listeners to be something fixed, to be so of the moment that it creates a platform of stability within it, but then it too changes. What remains constant in all of this, like the earth and the sky for the man in the boat? Perhaps only the sending and receiving, the speaking and the listening.

141 All of this is to say that presencing is homotropic and that it is illuminated by an awareness that is, at its core, calm, intent, and heartful. Homotropic here tries to indicate a superspatiality; if we go from a point awareness to a spatial awareness, when this spatial awareness in turn reflects upon itself, it sees that "space" was only ever a device to uphold the topology of the point. It can then naturally realise itself as homotropic—that is, the same in every spatial/non-spatial, temporal/non-temporal articulation. It says more, however. In many ways, this very refined understanding is only needed in order to illuminate being in a body, being a body, or being embodied; living the body's time and space, being so interfused with this nervous, electric machine of blood and muscle that each one of our thoughts carries an aroma of the kitchen or the sick room or the love bed. This body, which is spread out in subjective anamorphosis around the tiny doorway of the present moment.

142

Some words that are said arouse a hurt. How is this possible? The point of the hurt is not initially in the forefront of consciousness; it is part of the area which I think to be already secure, so that I can stand where I do in relation to what comes. As if one of my support team is suddenly knocked down. Their usual function is to monitor what passes and to deflect any possible threat in it by anticipating it; they are like antibodies, and their overlapping scope is uneasily reassuring, most of the time. When one is flatly contradicted and falls, there is a pull of energy back towards where it stood and away from the focal plane of present awareness. Creativity is needed to repair the loss. In the resulting distorted field, emotional thoughts arise recurrently; each is like a play or a movie performed in relation to a missing first person. The planning mind is drawn to this scene in order to use these simulations to secure a way to a future restoration of equilibrium. The protagonist of these plays, as projected forward by planning, is the putative self. Since it can have no direct sensory or synaesthetic evidence, a bodily feeling around the heart is enlisted as a proxy for it.

The body feeling is always the place where subject just was, the seat still warm as evidence that there really was someone there just a moment ago. This complex temporal structure is the play of mirrors that makes the subjective sense of pain so vivid, as if the clarity of consciousness could be scattered and dull.

143   When we look closely to see what is taking place, we are no longer in what was taking place, but in this looking, and the scene that now reveals itself is guided by its "taste" for certain kinds of unveiling; it is a sort of striptease of the mind. In the same way, there are certain topoi of the understanding as it faces onto inwardness, and it is not any conformation of ourselves into one of these that we seek to express, but the conformation of conformations.

144

Cancelling with preservation, or sublation, is in fact a triangulation. The first two or more terms do not have to be antithetical as such, merely different and yet of the same level, so that, seeing them together, we are forced almost out of embarrassment to move to an unsuspected level that encompasses both. Cancelling without preservation, which Eliot Deutsch calls subration—the movement of collapsing an illusion, as when the snake is seen to have been a rope—is also an expansion of comprehension, an awakening to, but this time unprovoked, and perhaps unprovokable by contradiction.

145 Between these paragraphs, there are numerous invisible paragraphs that express in eloquent ways the belief in the impossibility of writing. What ends up being written always exists in context of this invisibility. It is not only that the visible and the invisible enable each other, but they speak of each other as well.

146

This, the patent word stream, gains its full sense both as act and product by its relation to a silent questioning, an inexpressibility, a mute stress of physical being. Otherwise, to assimilate the words to life (as, say, expression) is to equate life with the strange death-in-life of text. Another way of saying this is to claim these markings as human signature. It is not about the self who is the agent of some moment's unsuccessful pull to master itself, but about the life diffused selflessly and equally across all the various pulls that meet in this moment. These include a heaviness in the belly, and the sound of my children's voices, and the look in a woman's eyes as she faces me, and time itself in all its dimensions.

147

Sometimes it so happens that I say in my heart, "This is good." These occasions neither refute nor embrace the rushed quality, but they augment it because they leave nothing for measurement when measurement, in its turn, comes. As if at one time I could find a home in this passing goodness that sealed my kinship with the world, but now it is the sharpest portent of homelessness, because I see that even my heart will not accompany me all along the way that I am going. The heart is filled with this goodness, but the eyes are fixed on another horizon.

148

When a movement happens deep in the core of my being, like a shifting of the ballast in the lowest hull of a ship, it becomes clear how little any willed or planned suspension of spirit can reach that *adagio e sostenuto* which is the long-sought counterweight to everything that is known about life. Below all decks is below the diaphragm, below even the rumbling of the engines to where the true basso resides. What sweet words could I find which could slowly withdraw and point the way to the silence wherein this ever-present sound is heard?

149 Observe the habit of the mind which re-creates this sense of itself erect and salient within the known and inflowing world. A certain commentary is maintained in which I am distinguished by my wit or quirkiness or even by the readiness with which I absorb contradiction, and there is a gentle reflection of this commentary which witnesses its uniqueness, as if I am in need of formal definition. This is a defensive constitution, sophisticated enough to absorb its own undoing (for the most part), an undoing which is posed in the form of an encounter with a stronger formal uniqueness in an other. We play this game, and different teams gain possession of the ball and score or fail to score as time passes, but no one ever becomes the ball.

150 What is it to be filled with a strong emotion that cannot readily be described? And what can be said in the midst of this about the kind of consciousness on which it arises? There would be less interest here if it were not for the utter indifference to commentary that is integral to it. The possibility of bringing this into relation with truth seems utterly gratuitous, *verum* is so obviously *factum* that we see that it doesn't refer to anything but the cult of the process which brings it about. The emotion is a rival process; in gaining precedence, it shows that the scope of the subject may be limited to the narrowest range of feeling without in any way diminishing the essence of subjecthood, to use a clumsy phrase for what at other times, say, grounds the realm of truth in own-being, and with just as much obviousness.

151

At this stage, what embodies the personal tone that recurs in these words is not the content or even the target, but the attack—the precise degree of predictability or the gently resigned tone of the analysis. What we call "identification" is analogous to this; it is a music of the body within, but not wholly absorbed by, the music of the world. For this to be of any use, we must ask what are the minimal conditions for the hearer of music who experiences not only ideas of order, but the will inherent in temporal form to impose itself in repetition and in unending variation?

152 As long as there is some sort of dialogue within consciousness, there will always be this paradigmatic shifting and circling—themes and variations. Even where a maximum of signification is occurring, the mind cannot help dancing with itself. Consciousness is equated with the most lucid maps of reality, but the insight that these fail utterly does not appear on any map. This is old news perhaps, but the implications of that non-appearance are still hotly contested.

153 At its most earnest, humanism emerges out of Christianity because of a suspicion of a lack of gravity in the notion of an afterlife. In the end, the meditation on death—which contemplates the surrender of transcendental consciousness as well as of personal consciousness—leads into a post-humanism. Here, extreme passivity—an intellectual image derived from the fact of the corpse—is given an always-paradoxical sovereignty. It is a strange and sophisticated mutation of the cult of the thing. The post-humanist face of the Other is only revealed in the dead body, or one of its rhetorical stand-ins. So if a certain thinking pairs Kant with de Sade, then the same thinking could pair Levinas with the Serial Killer.

154 The understanding of understanding is limited; there is no touchstone of truth in it. We can scour ethics, epistemology, psychology, or even mathematics for solid premises to ground the proof of transcendental consciousness, and it is in vain. Similarly, nothing in everyday life necessitates a separable witness consciousness, and the evidence from neurology further erodes any probability of such. And yet, what of the consciousness that requires no proof—that cannot be found because it is the seeking itself? At least see that it conforms to none: none of the conditions, none of the truths that accompany any logic whatsoever.

155

As if attention has become charged with static electricity, it repels itself; it won't gather, but moves within kinaesthetic space from one frayed excess to another in that nervous illusion of wind. This is the counterweight to those internal states celebrated as self or soul. It is convex where they are concave, not allowing anything to dwell: no voice, no presence, no vanities of being or of representing the unaccommodated one—the original one whose physiology would register the traces of the path travelled. In essence, just as much this as the other, because embodiment is to be traversed by innumerable paths, questions, answers, reflections, and interpellations, which weave twisted and non-recurring courses through every mode of givenness and obliquity.

156 We can say that there are positive and negative selfhoods; they are different economies of consciousness and they have different theories of the self, since that is part of what a "selfhood" is. There is a flow of states and instances in the body and the heart and the mind, and these "selves" are temporary stabilities that appear therein, maintained by all the ruses of quasi-reflexivity, something like that. We can say "there are" or "there is" ... whatever. The problem is already in this "there are/is." We can attach it to everything, like Kant's "I think," but that is a kind of retrospection. In immediate experience, even the simplest feeling in no way falls under a simple "is." This is not to empty it, but to see that it be neither emptied nor filled.

157 Leaving the cinema this afternoon after attending a matinee with my children, we drove along a diagonal road straight towards the sun that had emerged from clouds low in the sky. The road was wet and the reflection was such that the entire length before us was a blindingly bright path of white light. Cars ahead of us shimmered and melted in silhouette, seeming to float gently in that no longer retinal space. It was sufficiently unusual to be remembered—not so much portentous in itself as a pointer to some other submerged possibility, another pointing, another pointing indefinitely. How do I begin saying the truth without changing anything, without any sort of position or imposture of knowledge? Everything already said is to be abandoned, yet one does not entrust to the moment but to that which lies far below it.

158 *E fango è il mondo.* There is nothing closer to the core of this writing than the closure of every mental path, the nausea of interest that now prevails. This is because there is nowhere to move to and duration is experienced as pure tension, unbearable in itself and doubly unbearable in any attempted slide into mitigation.

159 If it were possible, I'd draw the attention of a reader to what the small blank time just before the first word here stands in for. Waves of tension building up in which no one can speak, in which there is only the scandal of my non-existence, my implosion after the mechanical reflexes of a history of earnest subjectification. Oblique, deferred: the momentum of these living moments in relation to the haven of a subject, of some sort of voice that would begin. This voice never begins in spite of the fact that words start to come, dedicated in their effortful way to giving some sort of expression to the paradoxical middle space between two contradictions.

160

Desire is a movement in being which does not subjectivise, but which is always the intense expression of a possible subject, or of an inaccessible one, or of a destruction of any possible subject. Who would there be (here) failing any attempt to wear desire like a glove, or to be the perfect glove already for desire? And what sort of subject is it that invests so much in the sublimity of desire, confident of regaining himself on the other side of each violation, even with no memory?

161

Your life, his life, her life speak to me directly and without articulation. I hear you in the very wound of my own life, or else in its gentle abandonment. In this way we are always and already intimate prior to the defensive perversities of will that make us citizens of the psychological world. We are unaware of this soft world with its insistent tendrils, if we are unaware of it at all, in the way that we are unaware of a large and determining material reality, not like some soft sound drowned out by the noise of traffic. And yet, this place of deep intimacy is also, paradoxically but by its very nature, a place where truth and untruth, sincerity and betrayal are indeterminate.

162 In a reflection on the thoughts that successively paint the present moment in the course of a day, in a reflection which views them as from a future moment reduced to essentials, the possibility of numerous little openings of the true eye is projected in the little gap of conscious insufficiency that belongs to each scene. It is as though another consciousness is being offered, in which the future is redeemed from giving its heart to all this impermanence. Of course, one fails again and again to pick up the invitation, but that one is so interpellated by eternity still serves to justify the project of the present. The insufficiency one would like to court in this way lies at the far end of the understanding of the incompatibility of the basic terms of this whole story: present and future.

163 Mechanisms such as the ability to form "theories of mind" and "theories of physics" have evolved to facilitate survival in a social group, in both senses: survival as a group and within a group. It is a further and later development that this is turned around, that a "self" is constituted as the subject-object of all these exploratory categories originally directed towards a reality innocent of such a distinction. There is no reason to conclude that this is an illegitimate creation of mind, but as is the nature of such processes, it is an ongoing and slowly self-correcting project that, at any time, shows ample evidence of its own prehistory. Wanting to know myself-in-time may be just such an artifact.

164 This city is like a vast coral, it's myriad cells and chambers formed by the psychic projections of the even more numerous souls that have at any time taken body within it. In spite of all the cultural differences, this collective and intrinsically mythic life of the city imprints a sort of family resemblance on all of its physiognomies without lessening in any way the extreme quality of each individual expression. "What have they done with their lives?"—the title of a book in which each page is a face.

165 Cultural forms, whether traditional or newly invented, minor or fully articulated, no longer serve as containers or as scenery for a life. That is, it is no longer as if they are the relatively fixed reference points against which the dialectic of life could play itself out. It is certainly not that they have grown obsolete too quickly (because nothing becomes obsolete these days), but that they are themselves seamlessly merged in the no-longer dialectical movement that embraces subjective forms as well as cultural forms, and every context and meta-context that belongs to them. I can revisit the scene of a past epiphany and the interior movement, which renders the moment impossible to repeat, coincides with the external movement, which has destroyed the aura of that locus. Both have been replaced by other moments that meet in an anti-epiphany. The dialectic of life was to issue in spiritual certainty; what is it that this non-dialectical movement opens on to?

166

Poverty of spirit, willed but not chosen. Bare, I am unmoored from any selfhood. This is a surface paradox; only in the quickest moments of the waking self, knowing for a bright breathing instant that this is not a dream, did being stand open. And, having opened, the shells of past and of future—the mediums of self with its remembrances and redemptions—slowly break up and scatter into dust.

167 This I am which must be asserted at any cost and against all threats of usurpation—what is it? Wherever there is evidence of living light it will have already owned it, already been there; since it cannot do this at the level of content, it seeks to do so at the level of form. By my essence as the life of this life—the condition of any manifestation whatsoever—I already possess that self I see in you, which, at the level of content, is most painfully alienated. I am the bitter claimant to the priority of all sweetness, a trumped-up *droit de seigneur*.

168 An argumentative voice that makes no arguments: this is literature to the degree that it is the staging of a sensibility, or, more accurately, a family of sensibilities. As such, the poles that mark its critical range are passion, wisdom, randomness, naiveté, penetration, breadth, concentration, and so on. It makes itself alone the better to be intimate with its addressee, with its anyone in particular, but still it is performance by inadvertence and could not otherwise be the work it is. Need it be a work at all, however, since finally the only begetter of these words is that which is unchanged and untouched by them?

Bodying Forth (2002)

What

happens? And who wants to know?

"That birth and death alternate, that winter and summer succeed each other, that all things glide along and move is a generally accepted proposition. But to me this is not so."

Seng Chao

Is there anything in experience that can provide a basis for knowledge of what is ultimately real, or even of what is necessarily real for me? Is some sort of transcendental deduction possible? In Kant's time, the natural analogies for such a defence of experience were space, time, and mathematics, since these were at the heart of the most successful contemporary sciences. In our time, an equivalent notion would be information, or, more fundamentally, difference.

Experience

of difference exhausts the metaphysical content of difference. In other words, the concept of difference is based in experience but is a generic concept and so cannot be pinned to a specific type of experience. In this way, it may seem to be prior to experience. This logical vastness or depth does not, however, warrant the transcendental deduction that difference is ultimately real. How does one thread one's way from the experientially posterior to the metaphysically prior? The hoary old reflex that has reiterated this demand is of more interest than its solution.

If

difference were to be accepted as holding for the real, then we would be in a wholly discrete cosmos: ultimately, one of multiple solipsisms. This may be the case, but the imperative to keep this question open runs deeper than the links of a possible reasoning that would prove it to be so. Similar problems beset a deduction on behalf of any experiential counterpart of difference, such as "oneness."

Difference

is achieved strategically in relation to some end; this makes it actual. The world is developed like a film by solutions of appetite. The appetite for the real is like a developer that is too strong and erases the image. Whatever is posited strategically is always subject to revision; it does not support premises that go beyond its occasion.

Difference,

as implied in the indelible solitude of the self, is nonetheless immanently transcendental; that is, it is wholly immanent, but stands in relation to all other immanences as if it were transcendental, as if it did faithfully represent being. This is one experiential axis of difference; the other which unfolds as the panoply of the world is (seemingly) easily traced back to the self's ability to differ from and within itself—its ability to dream. Where these intersect, we can no longer speak of difference (nor of self) but must adopt a new word, such as "the open" (cf. the eighth 'Duino Elegy' of Rilke).

Whatever

may be possible as a logical or metaphysical deduction, the interest here is in an experiential deduction: to one lying awake in the dark, beset with a paradoxical demand—abandon everything that will fall away and find that which abides. This is a venerable starting point. To it we must add: to one lying awake in the dark, there comes the realization that we are always lying awake in the dark. Furthermore, the second half of the demand is not so unequivocal. Who, within us or beyond us, could ask for that which abides? To describe it in this way is to beg the question. In the dark, we are called, but we know not to what or by what or even where to locate the addressee of this call.

There

are other starting points and other inquiries, yet, even of the most pragmatic, there is a sense that they take place within the frame of the same inchoate demand. We do not imagine animals as sharing this same imperative, yet when we try to imagine intentional robots, they are subject to it, and, *a fortiori*, when we imagine ourselves to be such knowledge-hungry robots. We are impatient to uncover our own impostures, as if to do so would quiet the rage.

These

are observations about the imagination, but to say so requires something like the Romantic imagination. What fulfils this function in a post-Romantic era?

The

body-self and the mental "me" are two modes of self that I can distinguish and alternate between in exploratory attention. A very deliberate effort of attention is required because these different modes play the same role in the ongoing organisation of experience and cannot appear in that role at the same time. Still, the mental "me" can appear to have been the observer of the body-self, but not vice versa. They answer to being the standing realities or immanent personae of that functioning self which gives itself over to oblivion in each inner event.

It is possible, by a certain inner effort, to change the mode of attack of presence, and of the fading of the contents of perception and of sensation. In the same way, what is perceived outside the body and what is sensed inside it serve as events against which we construe differing forms of lived time. Examining this more closely, we may be inclined to subsume the content of perception into the general sphere of the contents of bodily sensation; we may do this without loss of transcendence since there is no possible limit to the forms of lived time. At any rate, the salient contrast is with (discursive) thought, about which none of the above is true.

Discursive

thought, then, is not distinguishable from the flow of lived time, which it indeed seems to fix in an unequivocal sense. Its grammar, in both implicit and explicit insistence, provides the topology of linearisation for that temporality in which we will always strive in vain to recover ourselves.

The most blatant form of discursive thought is silent inner speech, and this mostly has a more or less optional character. Even so, when we exercise the apparent choice to stem the flow of this speech, to halt the process of its forum, we merely still certain facial muscles and are able to sense that we have already acceded to the little bright sentential capsules that shoot from we know not where into the space of our attention. Regardless of this, at each moment, we find ourselves in an ever changing life situation; the colouring and the solicitations that it bears with it as it comes over to us are also discursive (although less obviously and less optionally so), and, by that very discursivity, belong all the more fatally to us. This incessant process where feeling and quantity of life are transformed into narrative is where we naturally, un-thankingly, find ourselves.

Narratives

arise in the space where other narratives break off. This breaking off is the appropriate mode of ending for any story, since it leaves the possibility open for resumption. Stories within stories, divagations, deferrals, multiple threads: forgetting or leaving aside is as much a part of this moment as resuming, as starting afresh, as gathering up into new sense. There is a resonant silence when a story breaks mid-sentence ... and then, another story begins. We are not sure if it is the continuation of the previous one or a new story altogether.

All psychological objectivities are cultural artifacts, nonetheless, and crooked as they may be, they permit us to dismantle the machine. Isn't this rather naïve? What you call dismantling is another artifact from the same tool chest, and the degree to which these yield to one another is already delimited. We may imagine other tool chests and other forms of penetration, but the fact remains that all awareness of the machinations of inner reality goads us to this task.

Working

with effort at the gymnasium, I become divided into two parties: the one that is determined to continue and the one that begs for a stop. Each of these is a possible point of identification, but in the moment I cannot entirely identify with either. For the most part, I am the former. This is the one that then becomes implicit; it commands from a bridge in the mind while the other keeps trying to break in from the side of the body. It is as if they are vying for the allegiance of the one who actually executes the actions that constitute the lived moments; the identification for this one takes places in an ongoing way. It is as if the "I" can only know itself through this process called identification—the reflexive accedence to one of the parties—and this knowing is not merely cognitive but practical; it determines its active choices. The reflexive choice cannot settle conclusively for either side since it requires a unity of meaning and feeling, and these are divided between the two. Again, the oddity of this process may be just a reflection of the neurological incompatibility of the two dispositional systems.

This

weariness at the end of a day in which consciousness is just a skeleton force—the wakeful reference to an "I" is discontinuous; the focalisation that is its special attribute is wandering and indifferent. Because it requires such deliberate maintenance, it is a zero degree of waking consciousness and should therefore be more revealing of its essence than the mind of noon. But this consciousness merged with feeling is contemptuous of words. The realm of interest opened here as writing seems to be panoptic, but it is virtually blind to the current of life which sustains it and which it worships.

Love

and emotion (like commitment and ease, or reflection and suffering) are not opposites, but dialectically related parties in the sense that they appear as reciprocal identifications. As such, they remain out of reach—each one blocked by its partner—and hence function as the vanishing points that define the more or less perspectival space of (human) experience. Wisdom is to learn their synthesis, which is no longer played in such a dialectical space. The terms are then realised as finite—infinitely fragile, but attainable. This finite is the particular fully exposed in its mortality. We live once. We have to choose. There is no system.

In the songs and stories that we hear or that we tell ourselves, emotion is so often evoked by love prevented that it almost seems to be identified with it. If self-love were to be included with love, it might be possible to argue that all emotions arise in this way; however, in the recurrent narrative mythos, love is very precisely defined as an opening towards the other, which may be narrow or broad, deep or shallow, depending on the context. However, the essential association with emotion that is added to love in these forms threatens the very possibility of such an opening. Love is a turning of the will, while emotions are a movement of feeling. It is only when the two are grasped as entirely separate that we may contemplate their synthesis. In Christianity, an entire faith is based on a narrative that confuses love and emotion. This may be the key to its greatness, but it also explains why the history of Christian love is such a chequered one.

In some fields of mathematics we actually encounter the phenomenon of an expansion of context in which a previously infinite term becomes finite. This could be a model of the spiritual and psychological phenomenon called transcen-dence, but it may show only that mathematics is in thrall to the same illusion. Looking in the world for concrete examples of this paradigm, we find that it is either so ubiq-uitous as to be banal or so rare as to be effectively non-existent.

The strong character is one that remains consistent in focus and direction in spite of the various reflections of it that are ascribed to others. This character seems to pre-exist its dealings with the world and to be founded on a base of knowledge. The weak character is one whose form is continually renegotiated through ideas of the world and which so lacks the constancy of anything to be known. The latter may, however, be more self-conscious than the former, and in this way constitute a deeper, if unreliable, point of knowledge, which is an ironic knowing of itself and the world. This is a thoroughly Hegelian antithesis (cf. his discussion of Diderot's *Rameau's Nephew*) but it functions as much on an intra- as inter-psychic level. We can find ourselves living it on a day-to-day or even hour-to-hour basis. Like a buoyant doll, the "I" always bobs upright in any sea. (See also the character played by George Clooney in the Coen Brothers' film *O Brother, Where Art Thou?*)

Each

moment of waking consciousness emerges from latent body awareness. In fact, it never leaves body awareness, but if it has any sort of career before mysteriously being superceded, it sculpts this plastic inner sense of materially being here into the appearance of those luminous and self-determined forms we call thoughts. When I am ill, it is as if the body remains asleep in all of this, and so my wakefulness is also moulded out of sleep. It is hard to believe that this is not just an exaggeration of the usual state of affairs: the flesh being almost always, almost everywhere enfolded in sleep.

The

sleepiness of the body is because the senses which constitute the life of the body do not themselves distinguish inside from outside. The body's intrinsic picture of the world is of a space defined by the evanescent saliencies of an indefinite mass of sensation, indefinitely merged with its own flickering movements and shadows of movement. (Possibility is, before anything else, a kinesthetic category.) This may often seem a sort of grey paisley world (and quite poor in comparison to the one called into wakeful definition by the imperious outside), but it knows many more dimensions of motion; in surrendering to it, we pass into dreaming—a state in which unlimited freedom is ironically countered by an almost total absence of control.

It

is possible to imagine an unending dream, but difficult to believe that an unending waking state could have any consistency. The diurnal cycle is not only a habitual consideration of waking mind (at least in its caretaker role), but seems to be intrinsic to the constitution of all psychic objectivities. The self is already that which expends itself so that it may renew itself, and even the perception of colour requires a screen that is continually melted down and started anew. The things that belong most thoroughly to the waking world have in them a sort of strain, as if they are pushed into unequivocal manifestation by a force that perishes in its very extension. In this sphere, everything is known through the body, unlike dream, where the knowing is entirely in body.

I am suddenly roused from a thick afternoon sleep and a split second later am aware that the phone is ringing. This tiny delay represents the time taken for the screen of reality to knit itself together, the response to the ringing phone presumably following more immediate pathways as a result of a lifetime of conditioning. For the rest of the evening, I am aware of the floating, constructed quality of the world. (It is no wonder that the ringing phone was used to just this effect in *The Matrix*). Again, on another occasion, I am dreaming I am in a room with loud music playing when the alarm wakes me up. I am aware of the alarm but I can also "hear" the music stop playing, as if someone switched off the sound a moment after the scene blanked out.

These

utterances are more or less successful at bringing this occasion to the surprising speakability of its origination—this occasion: as much that of this reading as this writing, although it seems as if a writer must formally present the shifter "this" to the reader. Consider it done. Being alive, being awake, are successive frames for this knowingness, which is the lighting of a multiply determined corner of a world. The perspectives implicit in these determinations belong, by definition, to a further inward transparency, but the constraints of the knowing (which are the parameters and ontologies of the world) can in no way reach there. Experience of the world and of the self apprises us of an extraordinary inconstancy, as if to gradually accustom us to thinner air, thinner objects, and surrender of the biographical knower. The events themselves draw towards a fuller satisfaction.

From

deep sleep, from dream, from immersion in the privacy of that syntax of afferent and efferent sensitivity known as the body, we emerge into this common space, this "clearing" where we meet and lose ourselves again in the endlessly interwoven threads of our lives. Mundane, quotidian, these words belie the miraculous consistency of this reality, so regretted by the dead Achilles when he is summoned by Odysseus. The medium of this knowing is revealed, in essence, when it is just turned within itself. This is the fluidity of dream and the flowing reabsorptions of sleep, and yet, rising to the surface, it becomes a world of recurrent mutual objects whose very changes are subject to strict laws of conservation. Whether this all reflects the odyssey of a point subject or whether subjective effects result from the activation of phases of an immobile reality, the possibility of an awareness oblique to the diurnal round is breathed like oxygen and turns all jadedness to wonder.

Every

moment is supremely open, that is its nature far prior to what we imagine could be brought out by any cultivation. This openness is, paradoxically, utterly private because it is intimate, with an intimacy that is the other face of its nature. It is not that the intimacy belongs to a subject; the subject is an hypothesis brought in as if to ground this intimacy, which otherwise seems to turn away even from itself. That Being simultaneously reveals and conceals is to be understood this way, and these indications of it which attempt to bring together primal openness with human spaces are themselves the openness of this indelibly mixed space.

There

are forms of sentience far subtler than consciousness, and which form the underlying field out of which it arises, like a flame playing over coals or a pattern of ionised gases in an electric field—more subtle forms of feeling with no clear boundaries, so that the momentary answer to the question "How are you?" is like the solution to an equation. (That is, a kind of trope which is neither metaphor nor metonymy, but which we know.)

How

can we even put this forward when it is only consciousness which provides the "there is" in which to situate the very possibility of such a field? Because we are beings who know sleep and falling asleep, when consciousness flickers out while feeling remains continuous, although undergoing an involution.

Thought

is separable from body, but not feeling. Even when feeling is transferred through music or song, it is always inclusive of a body sense with which it is not necessarily identified. The inclusion may be a function of the very impossibility of identification, as when the body sense is indefinitely plural. Thought as distinct from feeling is an abstraction, a passing to the limit, but this is just what thought is: abstraction, limit, infinite, functional. At other times, however, I have noted that some works of Bach seemed as if they could be enjoyed by beings with no bodily sense, as if there were purely intellectual or spiritual emotions.

The reference of feeling to an outer world seems to have a tension in it—outer world being counterposed to body-in-feeling—so that consciousness is work in some thermodynamic sense. I'm really asking why it is we need to sleep, why this need is pre-understood in waking consciousness. A state of supreme lucidity, where thought flows effortlessly, united with lively feeling, is one that we know to be transient—a subtle strain on the organism. The waking state that seems closest to indefinite extensibility is that of insomnia, which is one of fitful and incoherent feeling. Significantly, the closest we often come to the former state is in certain kinds of lucid dreaming or in creative bursts, when the pressure of the outer world, its gravity, is suspended.

A moment of consciousness can never be found; it is lived here and now, patently, and yet when we look for it, it is gone (so that it is always consistent to deny qualia). It comes to flower only in a gaze that looks through it. Consciousness, then, is the tenor, and feeling the vehicle, but we never intend feeling as such. Since feelings are not separable, to speak of them is to make distinctions in an ever-changing field, one that is multi-dimensional or a-dimensional. We know them, but we cannot speak them as they are known.

Do

feelings predispose a distinction of inner and outer, of within-the-body and out-in-the-world? Perception makes this distinction, although I would suggest nowhere more clearly than in the distinction between a dreamed space and the world in which we find ourselves awake. On the other hand, there seems to be no feeling that cannot be deepened and extended by acts that have the body as their sole locus. In the feeling of something "external", there is an intimacy with a counterpart that is known as other body regarding body. Aesthesis as inner feeling gives rise to aesthetic perception—an intimacy with "externally" stabilised qualia.

We might say that the distinction between feeling and perception is based on the fact that perception is merely qualitative and provisional of data relative to pre-given contexts, whereas feeling touches the thisness, the *haecceitas* of things, and is inseparable from its character as act, inclusive of subjective and objective poles. The distinction between content and act is somewhat off target, however, since what I am calling feeling is still qualitative. It is a matter of kinds of qualities, or of the kinds of attention that reveal it: the sense of being brushed by things, elicited, or that our inner elaborations of the experience are, so to speak, dialogic. We await the spontaneity of things. Openness is a comportment of (the act of) feeling, not of thinking or perception.

There

are two different mysteries in what David Chalmers calls the "hard problem of consciousness"—that is, the explanandum which remains after we bracket away all definable cognitive functionings. One of these is the qualia, the very feelings of what it is like to experience the world—any world. This problem is addressed by a two-aspect theory of reality where there is an objective outside and a subjective inside to things; it is amenable to a sort of "separate but equal" metaphysical apartheid. Any cognitively significant event is both causal (*de facto*) and specifiable in functional terms (*de jure*), and therefore the inwardness of things has no irreducible causal efficacy. The other mystery, however, is that it is the being aware of a world which makes a world; irreducibly, for me, the world arises within my knowing of it. This problem, which is difficult to state clearly, is what is addressed in those Quantum-based theories that attempt to connect consciousness with collapse of the wave function. Whatever the virtues of such speculations, they do address the conviction that consciousness makes the world to be.

We can imagine a qualia-giving consciousness that is still not quite a world-giving or ontological consciousness. This is why the nature of dream is so interesting. It is hard to imagine an ontological consciousness that is without qualia, although there is no quality per se of being. Nonetheless, the two seem inseparable, as in the following observations of Whitehead: "In awareness actuality, as a process in fact, is integrated with the potentialities which illustrate either what it is and might not be, or what it is not and might be. In other words, there is no consciousness without reference to definiteness, affirmation, and negation. ... Consciousness is how we feel the affirmation-negation contrast."

Would

a dreamer's consciousness be enough to "collapse the wave function"? It would seem not, since the dreaming form of awareness can register a situation without cancelling all the other possibilities. How about an animal's? Could Schrödinger's cat witness its own state of health? What about a human in a similar apparatus? In the absence of external evidence, can we witness the event of our own death? There is enough plausibility to the doubt to motivate the plot of a movie like *The Sixth Sense*.

The

ease with which we suspend disbelief for *The Sixth Sense* has nothing to do with intuitions about death. In this case, death is an allegory of art which, in representing beings in all their pathos, consigns them, and us, to a strange inter-realm—a life-in-death and death-in-life. This is, of course, all the more salient in cinema where we routinely view the preserved performances of dead actors. It is not possible, however, to separate the imaginary of art from all the other dimensions—social, linguistic, and ideal—that necessarily comport an imaginary dimension and which constitute us as human.

To be here as us, we represent ourselves to ourselves, whoever we be. This is functionality and feedback, and is true even of artificially intelligent systems. Such a structure cannot answer the question "Am I alive or dead?" since it can only interrogate an image of itself, and an image, by definition, is blind to this distinction. So again, is consciousness the bearer of an ontological dimension beyond functionality? Is it the witness of being?

Functionality

goes a very long way, as we are discovering all the time. Functionality plus embodiment goes even further and may even exhaust the ontological dimension of consciousness. Embodiment supplies specificity beyond specification. We know being in this way, and this is a being that has nothing to do with Platonism or other onto-theologies (although these arise from the mythologisation of this strange kind of knowing).

I am listening to a recital of a Beethoven piano sonata by way of a recording that was made 50 years ago by a now-dead pianist. My attention is mostly absorbed in the occasion of the performance, in which the pianist's sub-jective realization of the work is conveyed to me through endless subtleties of phrasing. More than this, it is the myriad decisions expressed in each moment of the per-formance, the very life of the performer embodied as irreversible cuts in the wax master, that I respond to, and through them perhaps also to the decisions of the com-poser. To realize all of this I must listen with my whole body so that it can lend its life, its irreversible passing, to these inscriptions. The medium of the recording flatly contradicts this quality of once and once only, yet faith-fully conveys it, but only to the degree that we can hear it.

Embodiment

is unimaginable. (This is why all pornography misses the point.)

The term "embodiment" traverses a number of contextual spheres, since it is a commonplace that the body is culturally relative. The larger contexts are where we are infinite and quasi-immortal, the narrower ones are where we are finite but still quasi-immortal, and only in the narrowest are we both finite and mortal. Of course, death too is culturally relative, but not my death.

Embodiment

is unimaginable. (This is why nothing we can know or remember or hope for can approach the reality of death.)

Some philosophers employ a thought experiment like this to show that our consciousness is not limited to this one organic framework: Imagine that slowly, and carefully, and piece by piece, the neuronal circuitry of the brain was replaced by functionally exact equivalent silicon circuits. There would be no point where you would be able to report a change, and yet beyond some point in the process, your consciousness would be realized by a quite different physical substructure. A very similar thought experiment could be employed to show the duplication of a consciousness, and yet subjectively this is absurd. There is no functional equivalent for the this-and-here that belongs to the body in its paradoxical unsubstitutability.

To wonder whether this is all a dream is not to look for evidence that reality has a dream-like nature, but simply to wonder whether it may not be revealed to be, in truth, quite different from how it has been taken to be. Evidence of how different in texture reality is from dream are of no avail precisely since we can imagine dreaming just such evidence and the conviction arising from it. To ask this question is to see how little we have to go on.

It is hard to imagine an animal with eyes that focus and that engages in complex and playful behaviour—such as a dog, a cat, or an octopus—that does not have a subjectivity, that does not experience qualia, or of which it is meaningless to ask, "What is it like to be this creature?" On the other hand, it is hard to imagine a robot or AI system that does have subjectivity, etc. Is this just a fact about imagination, or does it have something to do with the fact that in one case the consciousness is unsubstitutable while in the other it is not?

Many

of these questions reduce to this: Is consciousness a kind of thing in the world? This, in turn, reduces to the question of how we constitute an actual world for interrogation. And so on, around the circle again.

Unsubstitutability

is an ethical category; indeed, the presence of subjectivity seems to be presupposed in all ethical concepts, such as freedom, guilt, responsibility, reward, and punishment. Even ethical substitution, as in amends and the various ideas of transferred guilt or merit, is only meaningful in relation to a prior unsubstitutability.

There

is a congeries of ideas tacitly premised here on what, in another realm of inquiry altogether, is called consciousness. Even utilitarianism, seemingly the most non-metaphysical of ethical systems, equates the ethical substance with the capacity for feeling. Or, at least, for feeling happiness or unhappiness, which may be a further refinement of mere feeling.

It is almost impossible to imagine an ethical agent or object that is wholly lacking in the (potential) feeling of being itself. An apparent exception is the comatose patient who is given no hope of recovery. A utilitarian has no qualms about terminating life support in such a case, while a religious person may forbid it. The prohibition may be grounded in indirect ways on the possibility, in principle or in hope, of the patient's recovery, but it may also be a direct consequence of revealed law, "Thou shalt not kill."

Divine

law addresses us in our ultimate subjectivity, which is also our deepest freedom. Where a religious system is hostile to the concept of free will, something else serves for subjectification. It may be God's sovereign freedom (and our capacity to suffer or rejoice) as in Calvinism, or it may be our ultimate equation with the divine as in the Atman is Brahman of Vedanta.

Ethics

and religion may help to define the terrain of this inquiry. They are monuments off to one side or the other while this pursues the narrow path straight ahead.

The intuition that consciousness is freedom is reflected in another register in the "global workspace" theories, which locate consciousness in some central area of the cognitive mechanism having equal access to the results of all special processes. Here, what is essential is that the subject can hover over several alternatives before making a choice. Practically, freedom entails responsibility, which again entails judgement, and so we imagine the mechanism that enables it on the model of a courtroom. Or is the ubiquity of the court or deliberative council an embodied form of artificial intelligence?

Consciousness,

qualia, free will, etc. belong to a class of interrelated concepts which all have the property that, in searching them out, we only find reflections and allegories of our own seeking. This observation points to a topology, and hence to a kind of logic, that could provide a functional explanation for the persistence of these very questions; a logic of self-reflection can evade the paradoxes of self-reference, but remains maddeningly too simple for the philosophical imagination to grasp, and thence to find rest in. None of this lessens the mystery at any rate, at least for those who see the circularity in the very need to explain.

One

could say that the problem of consciousness marks the limit of explanation, but this is not quite right since an explanation of limit could still be called for. It is better to say that it is a switch point in the path of inquiry where it is possible to leave explanation altogether. A change of gauge: no longer any such thing, but this thing.

Explanation

is to spread out in a planar fashion, but this is exactly what is impossible when we are to include both the thing and the condition of possibility of the thing, object and subject, content and context. There is a topology in play but it resists us, not just because it exceeds our (physical) imagination—like a Klein bottle—but because we are ourselves inseparable from it. Nevertheless, a tremendous amount of ingenuity has gone into answering to this condition with some kind of interpretational act in which it is never enough just to invoke an impossible term; there must also be a doubling back of it onto the present act, a *mise-en-abîme* (to recall a once fashionable term). This move is a contemporary version of the cogito—a direct and momen-tary pointing to the untraceable this.

There

are no positive data of consciousness. To be aware of is always to be aware of being aware of, and there is no clear distinction between these layers. Even before it is perception, say, a consciousness is in meaning and, as such, is multiply determined. The phenomenologists, hoping to light upon a term for the most primitive move of consciousness, chose intention: a loaded and ambiguous word which pre-empted their turn to an interpretative and essentially poetic discourse.

It is not purely scepticism that leads me to deny meaning to consciousness, that would be to dwell on the indeterminacy of the distinction between dreaming and waking. It is rather, and here I can only gesture vaguely, the extreme disjunction between the present moment and the immediate past. Meaning, or a datum, is the past and is dependent on this: unknowable. (That which is cannot even be called Present except by way of the Past).

In the function of negation there appears to be at least a momentary affinity with reality. This divine discontent that wrenches itself free from any resting place, even from itself, may be motivated by a prior intuition of the real. But even without that, in its very movement it is in alignment as unknowing with the unknown. To assert this is, of course, to immediately betray it; it needs to be negated again, and the solution to this double negative is by no means obvious, although many have taken it to be irony.

Why

does irony fail? If it were a matter of falling short in some way then irony would succeed after all, in an ironic way. The answer is in that "after all." Irony is negation and negation of negation, but only after the fact. It does not derive from the negation that is presence, but from the negation of presence that enables position, from the flow of time. The archetype of irony is the contemplation of a past moment, or better, one past's "take" on another past as past.

Let us assume a Husserlian analysis of the present moment into noesis, noema, and noematic horizon. And let us further grant that these three terms are so inextricable and interdependent that we cannot draw the distinction of subject/object across them in any way; noesis is fused with noema, whose horizon is its enabling and material condition. Each of the three terms is prior to or subject of the others. Let us further say that, within this structure, the temporalisation takes place by way of the sequential relations of protentions and retentions, which are essential substructures of noematic horizon. This model seems able to elucidate to some degree the mystery of musical perception, or, more generally, of any durational topology. Why does it need to be so complex? Because it must strive to exclude the self-contradictory and belated idea of the flow of time.

What

do I mean by saying that each of noesis, noema, and noematic horizon is subject of the others—that is, stands in the relation of subject to the others as objects? Because the subject is always and with equal justice, pure (grasping) act, pure revelation of content, and pure latent and unchanging precondition for any act or event whatsoever.

The flow of time is necessarily belated, since it only refers to pasts. Present is not in the flow, but the flow itself is in the present.

Why

do we say "always" for constancy across duration, why not "all-whiles"? We implicitly admit that the flow of time is an accomplishment, the result of a certain method, or, better, of methods differently suited to whatever is current. The content of past and future is not being which is covered or uncovered by the flow of time, but it is made strategically in the fecund relation of content (*noema*) and horizon. There are ways to all of it.

I am trying to expose the implicit assumptions that give the world the taken-for-granted quality that it has. To expose is to doubt, all the more so because the intellect is contemptuous of what it understands. So I create a structure of doubt where there was putatively a structure of will and of "bad faith." If I am clever and do this well, there is a bracing and enlivening quality to it, but this structure of doubt is in its own way just as presumptive and artificial as what it exposed. In any case, there remains a feeling that it doesn't all quite add up yet, that infinite tasks remain to be done, that the "undoing" has just begun. In the way of structures defined by their relation to a vanishing point (which is indeterminately internal or external), nothing has changed at all. This is known as seeking.

I ask you for something and you refuse, derailing my expectation. This causes pain, and so I tell myself that I shall never ask you for any such thing again. I forget the pain, but my disposition towards you has changed. Later on, you let me know that you would now grant the same request, but I don't ask you again. Later still, I accuse you of always denying me this thing, and you retort that I never ask. In other words, the expectation continues but the expression of it and the aware-ness of it are inhibited. This is a miniature paradigm of the psychological self in which we can see that the same phenomenon may be theorised in terms of the unconscious, or of temporal horizons, or of social scripts, or of ethics, or language, and doubtless more besides.

Expectation

and expression can name two of the many cognitive subsystems which together constitute a "self-conscious life-form." (We project mechanisms like this onto animals as well, especially our pets, to just the degree that we imagine them to be self-conscious.) Taken as within a subject, each of these subsystems is in Time in its own way; if there is a lack of correspondence, of mapping, between different temporalisations, then we have all the phenomena that psychoanalysis ascribes to the unconscious.

The great theoretical antithesis used to be between structuralism and phenomenology, which, in turn, was the successor to body and mind oppositions. Psychoanalysis, cognitive science, and various theorisations of embodied and computational mind locate themselves in the interspace of these polarities. What all of these point to is that consciousness is no longer consciousness (it is never self-presence), and structure is no longer structure (it is never pre-given out of purely material considerations, but is as if teleologically determined by possibilities of knowing).

Consciousness

is not self-presence; so we try to think of it as other-presence in a scheme where an implied infinite (or indefinite) regression takes the place of self-adequation. Thus, "the subject is a signifier which represents the subject for another signifier" or "to be is to be the value of a variable." Other-presence is, however, just an antithesis to self-presence, or perhaps even just a mathematical transformation of it. What if it was clearly seen that the question of self-presence could never even arise? Similarly, the question of the simple being-here of "experience" could not arise, since it has no negation.

Sein

vs. *Dasein*. To be is not to be here. The latter expresses an implicit attempt to interpret being motivated in part by awareness of death. When one of us dies, he is no longer here; when I die, here will continue, but without me. But was there a here lacking me before I was born—is this what we study in history? No. The most we can say is that here is some of the flavour of being. We cannot speak, as many do, of death as "leaving the body," although it is clear when we look at the corpse of someone we have known that he or she is no longer here. This object no longer gives here-ness, and neither does it point to a *there*.

Death,

contemplated with its ineffable and inexorable gentleness, defamiliarises desire. We see how far we have strayed, how many layers of holding-on we have set within us, how it all must be traversed again in the opposite direction. What was it you wanted? This is an invitation to a relentless historical regression.

Death

constructs this as (a) life, and, hence, opens the possibility of history as truth, finding the origins of illusion, of sin, or of psychological or spiritual scission, whether under the banner of Freud or Proust or whomever.

We seem to shed skins frequently; or, better, we seem to act a succession of diverse roles in the slowly evolving costume of the body on the (usually) even more slowly evolving stage of the world. Seeing someone with the already natural gestures and language of a new station in life, it seems they have outlived their former self, but to us they carry their dead somewhere about them.

Like

the scenery from a moving train are the various articulated dimensions of personal history, running off. The slow moving mountains in the distance may be the body or society ... but here already the metaphor breaks down, since sometimes body and society are the most rapidly changing frames of all. The distant stars, the observer in the carriage—all are moving within themselves like the slow seething of clouds.

It is not a positive way that is sought, however, but with infinite deference, the practice of a subject that is, in the most local sense, the differential between knowing and realising heteronomy. This on the one hand; on the other, an open secret, a heterognosis, a realisation of anterior freedom without a subject.

Many

questions about the self founder on the limit expressed by the saying: there is no thing like what I am. This is as much as to say that what I am is not thing-like, and not a lesser being either, since, in as accurate a phrasing as possible, Am gives Being. Yet, the Am is ghost-like in a world of things. In some psychologies, the subject strives for the solidity and monumentality of a thing, and labours against its essential negation, but perhaps the nature of "thing" is constituted by us just for this antithesis, and so it can speak to us of ourselves. The way that things inhabit time and space is an endless meditation for art.

The history of a thing—a stone, a shirt, a song, an old tin can, or an axe that has had two new heads and four new handles. There is an endless catalogue of things and of modes of things, material or immaterial, originals and copies, dreamed and not-dreamed. The *res*, the matter, the real thing ... "Here's the thing." How naïve of moralists like Buber to distinguish a relation to "thou" from a relation to "it," as if the latter were somehow one-dimensional. The thing looks back at you (at least the not-dreamed thing does) and it tells you where you are, what sphere. Try getting a "thou" to do that!

Knowing

an other is like knowing in a dream—the object is inconstant and indeterminately compounded of one's own projections; it challenges, irritates, and evades so that the centre of gravity of subjectivity seesaws back and forth between the poles. Am I reading her, or is she reading me? Which of us holds the other hostage?

Autrement

qu'être. A thing cannot call me to account the way another person can, with their gaze, their attention, their listening, their silence. Animals ... well they are somewhere inbetween: dogs are easily fooled, whereas cows seem to peer straight into my carnivorous soul.

Is

"otherwise than being" the same as loving someone so much that you would die for them? I would give up my being for their being; this is something that is felt directly in passion, but it is not always so loving. There are numerous ways that humans love or worship certain objects or objectives unto death—a child, a nation, a god. This can be an immoral idolatry of the being of that object: that it or he may prevail. Death is an inseparable part of the imaginary of love, but isn't that, too, just an imaginary death, even if it passes to the act? The other-of-being folded up and waiting within being—that is hardly a surprise since we know what gives being.

Love

cannot be the basis of ethics, since it would be unethical to cleave to the good only as one loved the good. Love implies a choice that is seated in the marrow, but the ethical requires a choice beyond you, an Other's choice. Of course, the ethical imperative may well be "(to) love," but that is a different thing. Here, love would already be a test whose implicit, though unacted, penalty for failure would be death. All ethical imperatives marshal death, and in this way underwrite their law-like status. Even if the imperative was "survive," it would still, as an ethic, be directed to a principled survival, failing which, it would be better to die.

In love of another, the intentional object is the ethical substance of the beloved, almost as if to say: I love her because she is good. What is it I am calling ethical substance? Broadly speaking, the continuity of our actions and the world, the field of predispositions we generate in our forward motion, and that by which we implicitly put ourselves up for judgement. To love is then to will to intervene in the judgement awaiting the beloved. But this will is also culpable; the ethical substance is also that of the other, touching which, we render ourselves answerable.

This

is not quite right, since there is also love which is a will towards the other as merely being. Being, however, is a concept with no shape, so the intention to it needs to get hold of the object by some active force, namely its will to persist in being, which is already ethical.

To see the beloved, momentarily, merely being, stationary as it were in her essence, is to apprehend her in the inadvertency of ethical substance, in something she shows (us) in spite of herself while her attention is on something else. This is a great fueler of love, but it cannot be its entirety—at best: its ground, its drone, its bourdon.

The most potent inadvertency of substance is beauty in another, and acknowledging this helps us to see how the object, or lure of desire, is created by ethical substance. A purely passive beauty doesn't do it, but a beauty good, bad, proud, gracious, or indifferent does. The ethical substance provides the context for the crystallisation of the object of desire; it is almost a truism that the same woman (or man) excites us quite differently according to the context in which we come to know her (or him). The thing that we long to experience of the other and which drives us insane when we are jealous is the crisis of the will to the opening of themselves to us (or to him or her, the third person).

The beautiful object is neither disinterested nor does it seem inadvertent; it imposes itself on being, indifferent only to its creator or would-be possessor. This imposition is an analogue to ethical substance, hence the way that, to many people, the destruction of an artwork is a moral evil.

Does

what we are impose itself on being? It seems not, since we seek to do so by our engines or influences with such a failing success that we must always rebegin. We are not at home in being. If you touch the quick of us, we respond in too many modes, in all temporalities (punctual, durational, fictive, real), in too many to ever be contained in a collection, hence the futility of attempts to equate us, in any sense, to consciousness.

The ugly or kitsch object does not impose itself on being; it imposes itself on us as if we were (already) being and there were nothing more natural than to use us to get to being. This is a backhanded insult.

When

I see another human being, I see them with my whole body in such a way that, on some subtle level, there is a confusion of feeling and even of identity. Subliminally and spontaneously, my body reads and is read by their body, and a knowing is enacted in this way that is distinctive to personal relations. This may be mediated by the so-called mirror neurons, but phenomenologically it is more precise to say that where inanimate objects return my gaze, and hence locate me in metaphysical space, other sentient or personal beings absorb my gaze and so locate me in ethical space.

The

view of the self as immersed in a world continuously reconfigured by an enactive monism, the father of which is perhaps Merleau-Ponty, is seductive but incomplete. On the one hand, the immediate and non-dual knowing which it places prior to discursive consciousness has no warrant and is in fact often magical, or simply wrong. This poses no practical problem, since we have learned to use it only as the first hypothesis in a quasi-scientific enquiry, another of whose working premises must, of course, be radical separation and pluralism. On the other hand, it does not allow sufficient room for the symbolic, which, while entirely embodied in its own way, does not rest on any form of analogy, as for example in our primordial apprehension of sexual difference.

That

I seem to know the other, but may be completely wrong—this possibility rests on a non-phenomenological void that opens an ethical space, and also a space of desire, but these are hardly to be distinguished.

The non-dual imaginary may be regarded as the ground of compassion, and, hence, as an ethical space, but at best this could only be in a limited sense since it lacks an objective difference on which to found decision. At any rate, it is more immediately productive of mimetic desire: the most violent and self-enclosed desiring relation to the other.

The

late phenomenology of Merleau-Ponty carries a tremendous charge of revelation of the obvious, of what is more near than at hand, and it seems to resolve all conundrums of the subject and the object, etc.; this is not a philosophical revelation, but a poetical one. It unfolds what is latent in metaphor and in the deep joy at presence to a world; like Valéry's swimmer in *Le Cimetière Marin*, it answers core doubts with the wisdom of the senses.

"Why am I me and not somebody else?" If there is any sense to this question, then shouldn't it rather be, "Why am I me and not everybody else?" And is this the same as the meditational question: "I = me"?

"I"

and "me" are conventional designations with the peculiar logic of the shifter, in which they are part of a combinatory scheme with all the other pronouns. The moves that transform between "I" and "me" in this scheme are probably sufficient to generate the entire set; the move from "I" to "me" presupposes an interlocutor, a "you," and since the "you" is not anchored to the certainty of the "I" (or since you can say "I," but it is not my "I"), the "you" implies plurality, and hence a "he" or "she," etc. In the innermost consideration of "I = me"? "I" becomes interlocutor to itself—I view myself as if from the outside then ask myself what it is that I see. This is not quite as paradoxical as it sounds, since "I" designates both a term in the scheme and that for which the entire scheme is actual; it is as if the "I" is the player behind the mask of all identities as well as appearing as one of the identities (commonly known as "me").

The

moves in the linguistic scheme are indelibly phenomenological in that the choice of moves in a particular situation produces and is produced by the context, the understanding of that situation. I can regard you as you, or as he, or even as it, and I can regard myself as he or it on your behalf, or otherwise.

Self-inquiry

always remains a possibility, since no matter how subtle and encompassing our thought becomes, there is always an "I" term in reference to which the posited objectivities appear. This term cannot be assimilated to the world of these objectivities without losing its nature as "I"-subject, yet everything points back to its actuality, and hence directs a further inquiry.

We know, in a wholly pre-reflective way, a mutual coordination between subject and object. This accounts for the plausibility of Lacan's narrative of the mirror stage and also of all aesthetico-philosophical phenomenological monisms. Indeed, insofar as it too is plausible, it provides a better motivation for the indelibly phenomenological component of the pronomial group operations mentioned above. Closer consideration, however, reveals that this mutual coordination is, in fact, an inverse relation. The more weight is given to subject, the less to object, etc., but neither can be made to solely predominate in this way, as the cost of annihilating the other would be infinite. It is as if a constant is maintained in the mathematical product of subject and object, $s*o = k$. The constant k is, of course, not an absolute but a relative constant, and so we might call it a function of reality, $f(R)$. Thus, there is never an irruption of the subject (as in one interpretation of the mirror stage), but an irruption of reality.

We

can play with this derived equation s*o = f(R) in some interesting ways. First, we can combine it with the everyday sense of identity as expressed in "I = me" or s = o = self. The original equation transforms to (self)^2 = f(R), or self = $\sqrt{f(R)}$. This could, for example, be seen as justifying the humanist axiom that "Reality is (only) experienced in human relations." Such an interpretation, however, presupposes an incommensurability between a term and its square root, but if our field is the reals (in other words, if a certain degree of reality is accorded to all terms), then what we have here is a description of the way in which reality determines the self. The last of the equations above should actually read self = +/- $\sqrt{f(R)}$, reminding us that there are actually positive and negative valences at play. A term of positive valence is one that pushes back against another term with at least equal force: a negative valence is one that invites in the term that it meets with at least an equal yieldingness. Thus, a positive reality (waking life) gives rise to a positive or negative self of less certain valence than the reality itself, while a negative reality (dream life) gives rise to an imaginary self indeterminately negative or positive. (Mathematically, i and –i are perfectly symmetrical.)

In

self-inquiry as a spiritual practice, the equation s = o is replaced by its categorical negation, and one pursues every objective manifestation of self in the light of this. The only possible result is o = null (zero, empty set), which immediately implies that s = inf, so that our fundamental equation is now null*inf = f(R) (= finite reality). This seeming paradox is resolved mathematically by the theory of Non-Standard Analysis in which the null-term is actually a non-standard infinitesimal, and something analogous may obtain in spiritual awakening, at least to the degree that the very knowledge that any system of understanding fails to fix reality becomes productive of a whole new understanding of understanding, and a deeper immersion in reality itself.

An

enormous number of consequences may be drawn from the formulation in the previous section, not least of which is that the fundamental equation is now equivalent to f(R) = null*inf, so that all functions of reality are of the form null*inf, and, hence, "the sense of separateness" (which is a concomitant of finiteness) is a mere appearance on a relation of infinities (which, if not one of utter sameness, is not one of difference either). (Definition of infinity: something that can be equal to a proper part of itself.)

We

call the sense determined by $s = o$, and hence $o \neq \text{null}$, the everyday sense of reality, and that determined by $s \neq o$ and $o = \text{null}$ the awakened state. The s and o here refer to the subjective and objective correlates of self, and so while the former case is based on $s = o$, it is clear that this can never be directly experienced; it is a belief, or more accurately a lie, and one which must be sustained by tactics of deferral, denial and mediation, from which all of the psychology of the I-object can be derived. (In particular, its core anxiety.) The tactics do not include a knowledge of what it is they are defending against except as a sort of virtual point (death) masked by the same defensive negations, but the play of this virtual point in relation to the "life" of the I-object gives rise to a major element in aesthetic experience.

There

is no move possible for the subject of the everyday sense of reality to the awakened subject. As long as some form of s = o prevails, even, say, in the form s = k*o for large k, the key understanding is lacking. Systematically increasing k forms the so-called positive way, which can doubtless produce some spectacular results but nonetheless remains subject to the former dispensation under which any movement in s is also a movement in o.

The term f(R) as the relative constant—and hence finite function of reality—can also be interpreted as Limit or Law: that which necessarily determines the mutual relation of force and action, or intention and consequence, or of inner freedom and outer necessity, called fate. The concept of Law itself marks a junction point between subjective and objective realities.

The function of the mind is the practical anticipation of the world-lines of objective congeries—this is, as in the current orthodoxy, what has most survival value. The belief that s = o means that there must be an I-object, and so it becomes a concern of the mind, or rather its world-line does. Experiences of bodily emotions such as fear, desire, arousal, anger, pleasure, etc., are taken as clues to the wholly contingent fate of this object, and so the I-object, which is never seen, is contingently identified with the practical reference point of these emotions. I never identify with anything; that would be a logical impossibility. Instead, a variable, o, in an ongoing project—anxious concern for the fate of o—is conveniently identified with the object of another salient project—maintenance of bodily homeostasis, or surrender of homeostasis to pleasure, or the continuity of some objective abstraction, for example.

If

we place the proposition that there exists a self-object next to its negation—that no such object can exist—then it is clear that the latter is more true than the former. In a certain light, it abolishes it entirely, but the resulting state of certainty has no warrant to declare itself Truth absolute. Indeed, the being of such a creature may be ruled out by the same observation, since a possible knower being absolutely correlative to the known would be another self-object. Not truth, but reality—one is closer to reality, but only relatively so.

The
gears of dialectic do not engage; we remain in neutral.

The attempt to state a true philosophy must take into account the competing claims of structurally exclusive perspectives such as subjective and objective, individual and relational, etc., but the moment it relies on a schematism to hold them in place, it forfeits its philosophical basis since it has lost sight of the only philosophical question that remains—that is why and how are there such alternatives.

To think of different perspectives or realms as mutually inverse or conjugate views is one way to try to posit an underlying order to what seems an otherwise inexplicable diversity in being. It is a speculation directed at the most underlying law, but as it is also a perspective, it must belong essentially to one branch of the diversity that it seeks to compass; it can never deliver its ground to the thought which undertakes it, no matter how sincerely. The same limitation applies to every system of thought from Hegel onwards in its cunning ventures to include what it is forced to acknowledge as also un-thought. This is the same history in which philosophy begins to voice the demand to stop thinking.

Subject

and object form a mutual inverse within my experience when it is reduced to the essentials of solipsism. This does not imply a belief in only the self however, since by the very fact of enunciation, solipsism is intentionally inverse to relationship with an other. This openness to another haunts the very silence of being as much as, but differently to, the incorrigible priority of consciousness.

The limits of thought are thinkable, but they remain the limits of thought.

Hegel's

method is usually identified as the triadic dialectic, but in fact he plays this like a sort of cat's cradle on the combinatorics of the subject/object relation—is the object out there or in here? Am I out there or in here, since there is nothing but here, and here is only what could ever be there, etc.? In this, as in many succeeding systems of the actual subject such as psychoanalysis, a structuralism is in counter-point to a phenomenology. In contrast to this, there is the aspiration towards a pure phenomenology such as Husserl's. The value of the idea that justifies Chalmers' "hard problem of consciousness"—that there is a something which is just what it feels like to be experiencing x (Hegel's "sense certainty")—is that it is equivalent to the non-triviality of pure phenomenology.

The

phenomenon: that something shines and reveals a true facet of itself in the knowing which is apt for it. The substance of the phenomenon is the very knowing of it, and yet it bespeaks nothing if not the independence of the known. There is enough constancy in what is known in the phenomenon that inquiry can pivot on it and defer to a related or constituent phenomenon a so-called subject, however, the original phenomenon was all of a piece, if it was anything at all. Thus, what seemed to be on the side of the subject of one phenomenon proves to be another phenomenon of equal status but differently situated, and looking back we can never say that it was actually present in the original complex. The phenomenon is plural, but it is so by way of indefinite plurality.

Experentially,

the subject is a *horizon*-al phenomenon; logically, it is an impossible one.

The phenomenon is a way-station in the surrender of truth just before it disappears into the living stream of experience. Being true to myself, I acknowledge that it is just the positive feeling for life that maintains the sense of a spatialisation, a clearing, for the wonderful illusion of a truth to things themselves. The feeling for life, whatever its colour, is inseparable and dark and unreasonable.

The objective world is a subset of the subjective, and the subjective world is a subset of the objective. This is not a paradox; in mathematics, there is no logical problem with such a dual relationship, but insofar as one can be the cogniser of each of these conjoined propositions, one cannot be the simultaneous cogniser of both. Cunning theories can be proposed to overcome this, but they miss the point, which is just to see how the incompatibility points fleetingly to what or who has invested in a world which makes such questions possible.

The great idols of life, those marvels in which I hoped or dreaded to find myself: fear and desire, art, intoxication, derangement, sex, rage, serenity, bliss, contemplation, worship, history and the rest, or love, in which I seem to find myself in spite of myself … In the sober afternoon light, they are all revealed as artifacts in the common landscape of humanity, passages rehearsed over and over, symbolic coral. This sober light has its own not inconsiderable attraction: Where "I" was, there It shall be.

Most

subjective verities fall under the rule of the will-to-believe. We discover them, but only as sustained by a subtle and mostly hidden effort at bringing them about and keeping them there. This is like forgery, except that there was not some prior reality that these take the place of. There was nothing there at all; we are the sole authors of what we need, and it is the reality of the need that is shaped in this way into viable ideals. The more we are aware of the power at work in this, the less real the underlying needs are seen to be.

"**Meaning** is coextensive with significance"—this version of the pragmatist's creed may well be true, or even a tautology, without entailing that there is a complete corresponddence between structures of meaning and of significance. To view some area of meaning as textual is to see that it is based upon a play of material signifiers, but this does not imply that the relations of meaning within that field are guises for the relations of signifiers, or even that they are in some way reflections on the failure of such a correspondence. In the end, what is at stake is the licence for interpretation, and the point is that semantics or semiotics cannot underwrite the extension of such a licence, but only make us doubt that there could ever have been bounds.

"It's

gone, it's gone!" So much so that I'm unable to say what it is that has gone. Weeks on end with no questions and no surprise. What do I know? Who is it that would be compelled by the knowledge of death? What speaking position to open? It is good not to know, or to seem to know that it doesn't matter who, or how, or in relation to what I sink into the moment as into a warm bath.

This

track, this desertification of the subject, is the furthest reach of only one kind of truth. It lies in a landscape almost entirely undiscovered, so that one thinks of cutting across to other places on the periphery when the empty sky becomes unbearable.

I am a history and a climate reflecting that history and roiling with its mismatches and soured appetites. I am a multitudinous overlapping community of partial selves, reactions, mirrors, mimicries, and masks realised in demands and silences of the ever-changing moment. I am this fatigue, this vague nihilism of failed self-knowledge, this mildness, passivity, clouded curiosity, skeptical absence of a soul. I am what precedes the effort to say "I."

"**No** more pictures." This is how Saul Bellow's elderly narrator in *Ravelstein* responds when asked for his understanding of death. But where pictures have once been, there remains always the possibility of further pictures; the pictures are less real than the screen on which they appear. To put it another way, the ontological status of possibility is such that it cannot be swept away like phenomena. And hence, there is a rigorous separation between all phenomena and what can only be indicated with the words possibility or principle. Action or passion of the subject is this separation.

The white cinema screen is the pure possibility of all individual movies, but we cannot say that all movies—past, future, real, imagined, or unimagined—exist in some sense in the blank screen (although such a fantasy may be useful to an artist). It is rather that the screen—and the spectator—are unchanging realities that condition the unreality of the ever changing photoplay. The diegetic possibilities which make the meaning of the show are underwritten by the pure possibility inherent in what is always empty. Again, one can say that the movie was never really about the doings of the characters in it, but only about the life of the spectator, of which there has never been but one.

I cannot say there were no pictures before I was born, because there was no time, or there is no memory—two statements which are not exactly equivalent. At most, I can say that the phenomenological colour of having-been-waiting forms no part of my earliest memories. Similarly, neither does the sense of a transition of the subject; rather, it seems as if the subject came about together with the crystallisation of the inner time sense. Is the subject like the character on the screen? No, because he carries within him his own source of illumination—a *cogito* that twists aside all forms of mapping. Is this like a battery, running on derived power, or is it a source in itself and hence identical with the one source by the strange logic that obtains there?

To sketch out the subjective logic of an event, as I have been doing with "death," is an exercise in the imaginary in the broadest sense of this term. To this, it could be answered that death is a collision with the real and so is beyond any categories of imagination or thought—except that I have just evoked a category, the real, for what is outside all categories. That the real enters into thought, in the form of death, of ultimate material exigency, can hardly be denied. It functions as a term for what is outside all the other terms, which may be phenomenologically or logically full; it casts a shadow over them because it must remain radically empty in these respects. Death prevents me from invoking any Parmenidean identity of thought and being, but it does so not as third term on a par with these, but as an infinitely gentle, infinitely devastating irony.

Some

discoveries beg to be shared even before they have been fully considered. They may be no more than pretexts for an imaginary sharing, which is itself a way to buy off the others, to misdirect them, so that I might return to the real inquiry which is solitary and shuns communication.

The real inquiry, or the inquiry into the real, is a race with death, and so also a race towards death. One cannot say that it is of any interest, since the interesting is what arrests the flow of time, like an eddy, and creates a habitation for a picture of me within a picture, circling gently until it is swept away again. To meditate is to practise dying, or indeed to die as much as that can be an action, because it is to surrender everything that has been gained by interest.

> # What
>
> role is played in the constitution of experience as being that of a self-of-moment-in-affairs by the possession of deep time? This is the time of forgotten memories and intimations from childhood; it is what may be reawakened in epiphanies of the sensory world, what may suggest Archimedean regions beyond the flow of passing time to a Proustian sensibility. My vivid but infinitely distant sense of early childhood, and the conviction that it is the very same nameless Self questioning the dream now as then—an identity so emphatic that now and then become of one nature—forms a quiet but vital part of all my personal memories. And yet, it seems more an artefact than a datum—the very mechanism of memory seen in a certain angle of the light—because the content of the memories matters less than the way they are recalled.

The

indelible scandal of sexual intercourse is only due in part to the series of taboos that must be broached in initiating the act. A detailed description of these could be quite lengthy, but the essence is perhaps the willing replacement of our highly developed sense of respect for the other in their personal integrity by a violence of desire that disintegrates them and us into a succession of a simultaneity of parts, both sensual and moral. And yet, on the other side of these transgressions, we re-emerge within a world that is unequivocally good. "Imparadised in one another" is a phrase that has often come to mind for this state, and it indicates as well the exclusivity that is the remainder of the scandal. The social sanction that various forms of coupling receive may be significant, but it is the phenomenological exclusivity in the act itself that I am addressing. Two (or more) people engaged in making love have momentarily broken their social contract with the world; their bliss is uttered in a private language so that when it is over, even they will be unable to locate the referents.

The breaking of a heart is the most excruciating goad to transcendence. The love that was ignited in a nucleus must awaken to its inherent disinterest if it is to survive in that shattering pain, because that is the only way it ever could have meant, even when it was exclusive. What happens to the scandal then? If anything, it becomes even more shameful. We avert our eyes from one made holy by suffering, as if everything excessive, everything exclusive, everything peremptory now has designs upon us.

Select Bibliography

Beckett, Samuel. *Proust*. New York: Grove Press, 1972.

Beethoven, Ludwig, van. Piano Sonata in B flat major 'Hammerklavier,' Op 106, III. *Adagio sostenuto, appassio-nato e con molto sentimento*. Performed by Solomon Cuttner. EMI, 2005.

Bhattacharyya, K. C. *Search for the Absolute in Neo-Vedanta*. Honolulu: University of Hawaii Press, 1973.

Brockman, John. *Afterwords*. New York: Anchor Press, 1973.

Chalmers, David J. Facing Up to the Problem of Consciousness. *Journal of Consciousness Studies* 2 (1995): 200–219.

Damasio, Antonio. *The Feeling of What Happens: Body and Emotion in the Making of Consciousness*. New York: Harcourt Brace, 1999.

Deutsch, Eliot. *Advaita Vedanta: A Philosophical Reconstruction*. Honolulu: University of Hawaii Press, 1980.

Dōgen, Eihei. *Shobogenzo: Zen Essays by Dōgen*, trans. Thomas Cleary. Honolulu: University of Hawaii Press, 1992.

Frieden, B. Roy. *Physics from Fisher Information: A Unification*. Cambridge: Cambridge University Press, 1999.

Jackson, Laura (Riding). *The Telling*. New York: Harper & Row, 1973.

Leopardi, Giacomo. *I canti* [Sec. xxviii, 'A se stesso']. Bologna: Licino Cappelli, 1835.

Maharshi, Ramana. *The Spiritual Teaching of Ramana Maharshi*. Boston and London: Shambala, 1973.

Michelstaedter, Carlo. *La Persuasion et la Rhétorique*, trans. Marilène Raiola (Paris: Eclat, 1992). [English translation, New Haven: Yale University Press, 2004.]

Seng-Chao. *Chao lun: The Treatises of Seng-chao*, trans. Walter Liebenthal. Hong Kong: Hon Kong University Press, 1968.

Stevens, Wallace. *The Collected Poems of Wallace Stevens*. New York: Vintage, 1990.

Whitehead, Alfred North. *Process and Reality*. New York: Prentice Hall, 1979.

www.ingramcontent.com/pod-product-compliance
Lightning Source LLC
Chambersburg PA
CBHW030817190426
43197CB00036B/508